SUCCESSFUL
SMALL CLIENT
ACCOUNTING PRACTICE

SUCCESSFUL
SMALL CLIENT
ACCOUNTING PRACTICE

Carl S. Chilton, Jr.

PRENTICE-HALL, INC.
ENGLEWOOD CLIFFS, N.J.

Prentice-Hall International, Inc., *London*
Prentice-Hall of Australia, Pty. Ltd., *Sydney*
Prentice-Hall of Canada, Ltd., *Toronto*
Prentice-Hall of India Private Ltd., *New Delhi*
Prentice-Hall of Japan, Inc., *Tokyo*

© 1976 *by*

Prentice-Hall, Inc.
Englewood Cliffs, New Jersey

Eighth Printing . . . . . November, 1979

Library of Congress Cataloging in Publication Data

Chilton, Carl S
  Successful small client accounting practice.

  1. Accounting. I. Title.
HF5635.C55 1976   657'.9042   75-20090
ISBN 0-13-872556-X

Printed in the United States of America

About the Author

Carl S. Chilton, Jr. has been a practicing certified public accountant since 1951. The three offices of his firm are located in communities of under 100,000 population and serve many small clients.

He has been a frequent contributor to the Practitioners' Forum of the *Journal of Accountancy,* and served as a contributing editor for the Prentice-Hall "COMPLETE GUIDE TO A PROFITABLE ACCOUNTING PRACTICE." His articles have appeared in "The Fish Boat" and the "Southern Pharmaceutical Journal."

He has served the Texas Society of CPA's as its vice-president and as president of its Educational Foundation. A charter member of the Southern and Western Accounting Group, he has been chairman of its Executive Committee.

He holds a business administration degree from The University of Texas at Austin, and prior to entering public practice, taught accounting for three years at Texas Southmost College in Brownsville, Texas.

A Word From the Author

Almost all accountants serve some small-business clients; many specialize in them. Servicing them effectively is the central theme of this book.

Often, small clients have problems similar in scope to their larger counterparts. The difference is they are more dependent on the outside professional for a wider range of services to meet their needs.

This book lists many practical ideas and suggestions on how to provide better accounting services while increasing practice income. It contains over 40 exhibits plus time-tested ideas for solving a wide variety of problems, giving the reader a wealth of information that can be used in his/her own practice.

Not only are the techniques provided a product of 23 years of personal experience, but a good deal of material has been gathered from numerous other firms and is used with their permission.

The first five chapters tell *how to organize for effective service.* They give solid advice on how to set fair and adequate fees, suggestions on being responsive to the varying needs of the small client, stress the need for effective communications, and provide valuable tips on development and management of a top-notch accounting practice. The advantages of having a broadly based practice are pointed out, stressing the place of small clients in building a broad base.

The second group of chapters gets right to the heart of serving small clients; *designing the accounting service to be offered.* Providing bookkeeping service is covered extensively in Chapter 6, which discusses different methods of performing the work, complete with exhibits and discussions of various systems and time-saving pointers. The special problems and opportunities arising from auditing small clients are highlighted, while another chapter provides ideas on improving accounting systems and office procedures. This section concludes with a thorough discussion of various types of tax service. Preparation of returns is discussed, as is the importance of tax planning and tips on handling a tax examination. Handling the workload and effective utilization of time during tax season are valuable features of this section.

The final group of chapters moves the accountant into a high level of service:

helping with business problems and profitability. Assisting with budgeting and forecasting is covered in Chapter 11, followed by practical suggestions for helping the client solve his financing problems. Finally, a wealth of suggestions for providing a variety of special services alerts the practitioner to both the opportunities and pitfalls in this area. Concrete suggestions are provided for organizing the practice to perform special services successfully.

Special emphasis is placed throughout the book on *effective communication.* The small client not only needs a good accountant, he needs one who can clearly communicate what the figures mean. Examples are provided of communicating through client newsletters on timely subjects. The reader will also find exhibits of financial statements with interpretive comments and special material which helps the client understand the figures.

Another point stressed is *the need to keep up to date.* The practitioner is cautioned against keeping his "nose to the grindstone" all the time. He is urged to attend meetings and seminars, exchange ideas with other accountants and generally to be aware of developments within the profession. As various phases of client service are discussed throughout the book, current developments are high-lighted and suggestions are made on ways of keeping up to date.

Good management of the accounting practice is stressed. An accounting firm cannot grow without good management, which is too often neglected by the busy practitioner. The need to devote sufficient time to management, the forms and techniques for planning and controlling the practice and the importance of appointing a managing partner are all discussed.

A budget for the accounting firm is stressed in Chapter 11. This useful tool is fully as important for the accountant as for his client. Specific suggestions are provided for budgeting various elements of the firm's income and expenses.

The accountant's success is determined in large measure by his abilities in *human relations* and *client relations.* This area is fully discussed, with examples of letters and various techniques for dealing with different types of clients and a variety of problems.

The message of this book is directed toward all accountants who deal with small business—and obviously there are many in this category. The majority of accountants in public practice will find valuable material here, regardless of the size of their firm or their technical specialty. The subject matter covers all phases of accounting service. Accountants who are employed by small companies will find many of the chapters rewarding. Some may be employed full time, others part time—all will benefit from the ideas outlined. Accountants who are thinking of starting their own firms will find this material particularly valuable. Bookkeepers who are interested in bettering themselves and doing a better job for their employer will get many ideas from these pages.

Those who study these pages will be able to do a better job for their small clients.

Carl S. Chilton, Jr.

ACKNOWLEDGMENTS

This project is a reality because of encouragement and help from partners and employees in my firm, as well as members of my family. My thanks to each of them.

The exhibits in this book have been assembled from a number of accounting firms. Their willingness to share their knowledge and experience is greatly appreciated.

CONTENTS

6. Keeping Books for the Small Client *(continued)*

6. Keeping Books for the Small Client *(continued)*

7. Auditing Small Companies: Tested Practices and Procedures . . . .

8. Improving the Small Client's Office and Accounting System . . . .

TABLE OF EXHIBITS

CHAPTER **1**

Advantages of
Serving Small Clients

Accountants have long wrestled with the question of what to do about the small client. Questions such as these are not easy to answer:

Should I provide bookkeeping service to businesses too small to
have a full time bookkeeper?

Can I prepare small tax returns profitably?

Is there any real advantage in taking on small clients, or are they
too much of a bother?

This chapter and those that follow take the position that small clients are indeed necessary for the building of a successful accounting practice. Take the following brief history of two accounting firms—a hypothetical case, but one that undoubtedly can be found in fact all over the country.

Our two firms started in the same city about twenty years ago. Each had two partners and a secretary. One of the firms decided to be selective in the clients they accepted and the work they performed. They refused to do bookkeeping work and turned away many potential clients who asked for this service. They established a fairly high minimum fee for the preparation of tax returns, thus effectively eliminating small returns due to the size of the minimum fee. They were also cautious in employing additional staff, making it necessary on occasion to turn down audit work because of inability to staff the job. After 20 years, this firm still had the same two partners and the secretary, plus two other employees.

The second firm took a different approach. They made an effort to serve every potential client who came to them. They felt that even the smallest client may grow into a large one and, in any event, can help bring new clients by recommending the firm. Write-up work was readily accepted, and the firm soon had enough of it to justify employing a woman bookkeeper. Small tax returns were handled with the understanding that the fee should be commensurate with the time and effort involved. Every effort was made to be responsive to clients' needs, to establish effective communication, to see that there was a sufficient staff to handle all the work. After 20 years, the firm had four partners and 12 employees, a well-balanced group of clients, and a momentum for growth.

What made the difference between these firms? The firm which grew obviously had certain ingredients that the other lacked. These could be described as enthusiasm, know-how in the area of practice management and a willingness to take on the problems of dealing with small clients. After 20 years, some of the firm's major clients were among those who had originally been small, but didn't stay small for long.

Successfully serving small clients is indeed one of the keys to the establishment of a growing accounting practice. Opportunities are waiting for the accountant who prepares himself to provide this service.

A Key to a Growing Practice

Any accountant who is ambitious and wants to grow won't be satisfied with strictly a small client practice. He wants some large clients with corresponding challenges and problems. How to get them? Take on small clients who have good potential for growth—some of them will become your largest clients in the future. In other words, grow with them.

In our practice the majority of our larger clients today started with us 15 or 20 years ago. One company that had 12 employees when we started serving them now has around 400. This assignment started out as a simple matter of helping the owner's wife with bookkeeping and now has become substantial audit, with unique problems and sizable fees. Several other similar illustrations could be given. Nor is this a unique experience—accounting firms all over the country can tell the same story.

Great Potential of Small Business

The potential in the field of small client service has never been greater than today. Small companies are of tremendous importance to our economy as a whole in this country. Over 90 percent of the firms operating in the United States are consistently classed as independent businesses. The U.S. economy is considered by many to be dominated by large corporations; actually over 90 percent of all firms are sole proprietorships or partnerships. Further, over 90 percent of all firms have less than 100 employees and have gross sales of less than $500,000.00 per year.

One noted economist has convincingly attacked the oft-repeated thesis that small business is on its way out. He cites the fact that the ratio of the number of business firms to each 1,000 persons has remained stable for 50 years. The number of business firms represents a general measure of new business ventures; persons ready to embrace the risks of ownership. The growth of big business appears to have been no faster than the growth of the economy as a whole, leaving small business with its own niche in a growing economy.

Thus, the accountant who envisions a world where small business is dying is operating under a false premise. Small business continues to thrive in our country and makes up a tremendous potential for profitable accounting service.

These companies cannot compete without good management. Good management requires full knowledge of the company's financial picture and problems. There must be an adequate set of books, current financial statements and sound financial advice. Studies of small business bankruptcies invariably cite poor records and poor financial planning among the principal contributing reasons. It is not surprising, therefore, that there is tremendous opportunity for accounting service to this group of clients. Many accountants today are building successful practices as well as making a significant contribution to the economy of their communities by serving this clientele.

A Broadly Based Practice

One accountant has stated that the ideal clientele resembles a pyramid. The practice should be built on a broad group of clients extending from a large number of small businesses at the base to a few large accounts at the top. A good practice is not top-heavy with a few clients so large in proportion to the overall clientele that the loss of one would be serious. The accountant serving a few large clients also runs the risk of not being fully independent, which impairs his ability to do auditing work.

Large businesses are not only few in number but they do not change accountants very often. You cannot expect to obtain new clients of substantial size with any degree of regularity. It is difficult to build a volume of business from this source. For that reason, the willingness to serve small clients is essential to the proper development of any accounting practice.

Practice Development

There is yet another advantage to having a large number of small clients rather than a few large ones. The more clients you have, the more they will "advertise" for you. Clients who have an on-the-ball accountant like to tell their friends.

Experienced accountants agree that the best sources of referrals are the following:

1. Existing clients
2. Bankers

3. Lawyers
4. Personal friends and acquaintances

There is general agreement that the number-one source is existing clients. The others will vary in productivity depending on the individual situation, but it is very rare to find an accountant who does not feel that existing clients are his best source.

A small client can be just as good a source of referrals as a large one—better, in fact, if he is enthusiastic. Some clients actually take pride in the amount of new business they can refer to their accountant.

In most states, certified public accountants and registered public accountants are not allowed to advertise or solicit business. Many clients do not know this. When they do become aware of this ethical limitation on their accountant, they are more conscious of his need for referrals. The wise accountant will let his clients know that he can't advertise or solicit, and that new business comes primarily from recommendations and referrals from present clients. The way in which we described this situation to our clients in a client bulletin is found in Exhibit 1-1 at the end of this Chapter.

One Point to Remember—When a new client appears at your office, try to find out where he heard of you. This gives you a better feel for where your referrals are coming from, as well as an opportunity to thank the referring party. It is good practice to write a letter of thanks if you won't have an opportunity to express your appreciation personally.

The Human Interest Factor

The small client offers a unique adventure in the field of human relations. You will frequently develop a close relationship and be in a position to observe closely the progress of the client's organization and feel you are making a definite contribution to his success.

In many instances, you will find you are the closest, and perhaps, the only professional advisor the client has. He respects your position and frequently shows a sincere appreciation for the service you are rendering.

Our firm has had the privilege of serving for many years a small merchant who came to this country from Europe after World War II. His family had been wiped out and his ability to speak English was, and is, still limited. He would never have succeeded in business without someone to keep him straight with the government. His appreciation of our service over the years has been voiced frequently and fervently.

Be a General Practitioner

In serving small clients you will have the freedom to operate as a general practitioner in the accounting field. Your work will not be limited to one particular area, such as auditing or taxes, but can range throughout all areas of service. This is not to say that you should attempt to know everything about all phases of accounting practice, since this is impossible. You must know where to go for expert advice at such times as you find it necessary. At the same time, your client looks upon *you* as his accountant and expects you to be able either to provide the service he wants or to know where to get assistance.

Locating Your Practice

Accountants choosing to serve small clients may enjoy certain freedom in the choice of where to locate the practice. It is possible to serve small clients effectively from a suburban location adjacent to a large city or to locate in a smaller community. In these days of major concern about the problems and hectic pace of urban living, some accountants prefer to practice in a location away from the city. It is true, however, that the city offers economic advantages and the challenge of working for major clients. There are, surely, no reasons why small clients cannot also be served from a city location. The choice of where to locate one's practice is a personal decision and, in many cases, the decision is based on where the accountant feels the opportunities are greatest. One of the advantages, however, of small client practice is the greater freedom of choice in location.

Conclusion

Serving small clients is not without its difficulties: there are pitfalls to watch for and problems to solve. These will be discussed as we go along. But remember that accounting firms of all sizes are willing to take on small clients. Some of the largest firms, in fact, have "small business departments" geared specifically to the needs of that clientele.

This much is certain: serving small clients is a rewarding experience, full of challenge and variety and rich in the adventures of human relations. You can enjoy the pleasant feeling of making a contribution to the well-being of your clients and your community. And, better yet, you can do this while adding to your own economic well-being.

<u>LONG, CHILTON, PAYTE & HARDIN</u>

CLIENT BULLETIN

PROFESSIONAL ETHICS

Certified Public Accountants conduct their practices within rules of professional ethics. Some of the more important provisions are:

(1) We are not permitted to advertise;
(2) We are not permitted to solicit clients;
(3) We are not permitted to own stock or serve as directors in companies that we audit;
(4) Every financial statement we issue must be clearly designated as "audited" or "unaudited" and must fully disclose all important facts;
(5) Our relationship with clients is highly confidential and must be so maintained at all times.

These rules are self-imposed by the profession. They guide us in our dealing with clients, with the public and with our fellow CPA's. The purpose of rules of ethics is to assure that public confidence in CPA's as a profession will be justified.

General knowledge of an industry or trade is helpful in our service to other clients in the same industry or trade, but we are precluded from using any specific information about any one client in connection with our services to another client.

HOW DOES A CPA GET NEW CLIENTS?

Our rules of ethics prohibit us from advertising or from soliciting clients. These are sound rules, since a professional service cannot be appropriately advertised in the way that merchandise is advertised. When people are looking for a professional man, they generally ask their friends to recommend someone.

Our experience has been that most of our new clients come to us upon recommendation of other clients. That is another reason we strive to give our present clients the best service we possibly can.

Exhibit 1-1—Client Bulletin Explaining Ethical Limitations on Clients

CHAPTER **2**

Providing the Service
for a Fair Fee

One of the principal concerns in the minds of some accountants is whether the small client can really afford first-class accounting service. It is true that he can't afford as much service or all the types of service as the larger client. But bear this in mind: he *needs* good accounting service and is better off with it than without it. If he needs it, he can afford it—and can ill afford to do without it.

It takes some skill to provide the small client the service he requires without spending more time than he can afford to pay for. You must be able to determine what service will provide him the greatest benefit—certain types of services may seem desirable but are not absolutely necessary. These should be postponed or dropped. The client and his personnel should be used for as much work as possible, limiting your own efforts to the most important areas. In short, provide the small client with service which is profitable to him and profitable to you.

An Adequate Fee Is a Must

The primary element in making the service profitable to the accountant is getting an adequate fee. Any fee arrangement which is unprofitable will, in the long run, hurt both the accountant and the client. It will be necessary eventually either to neglect the client or to reduce the level of service below that which he needs. The accountant is not only depriving himself of adequate revenue, but by undervaluing his services he is, in the long run, undermining his ability to serve and, perhaps, even his confidence in himself.

It has been said that a professional man should derive sufficient financial resources from his practice to be able to attract and pay a capable staff, to maintain a respectable office and adequate library, to have sufficient time to render public service for the community, to study sufficiently to keep up with developments in his profession, to maintain a standard of living that favorably impresses the community and to provide for his retirement. There is no reason these objectives cannot be met while serving small clients.

The ability to obtain an adequate fee comes from a combination of several ingredients. Self-confidence is probably the most important, closely followed by an ability to sell yourself to the client. These elements, plus learning the techniques and developing the "feel" of how and when to bill, all are the characteristics of an accountant who is able to obtain adequate fees and to operate successfully.

How to Set Fees

Successful firms use a formula as a guideline for setting billing rates; for example, an hourly billing rate should be 2½ times an employee's hourly salary. You can get about the same result by using 1¼ percent of the annual salary. Some firms go higher than this and some lower, but every practitioner needs a formula to guide him.

Once your standard billing rates are set, don't be afraid to give consideration to other factors in determining the fee to charge. Here are some things to consider:

1. Ability of the client to pay.
2. Future potential of the client.
3. Success or failure of the engagement.
4. Efficiency with which you handled the engagement.
5. Special value of the services.

Services That Command a Higher Fee

Certain types of services command higher fees because they require the highest of skills. These are services which the client is not in a position to perform for himself and where he must rely heavily on his accountant. One such area is the field of income tax examinations. It has been the writer's experience that most clients are only too happy to turn this over to their accountant—in many cases completely. I have had any number of clients request that the Internal Revenue Agent perform his work in my office and the records be made available for examination there. In some examinations, the client never meets the agent. All questions and answers are handled by the accountant and, of course, negotiations with the agent are conducted in the same manner. Clients do not know how to deal with an Internal Revenue Agent and many of them prefer not to do so. This is an area, therefore, where the accountant has performed a special type of service and should charge accordingly.

One of the natural fields in which accountants participate is that of helping their clients to obtain financing. Most accountants are more experienced in this than are their clients and are able to make valuable suggestions as to how and where to borrow money. Accountants are experienced in the preparation of financial information and other data that are needed by lenders and can advise clients what to expect in the way of loan conditions that might be required. They are able to advise clients and to be of valuable assistance throughout the entire process of obtaining financing. The fee should be set accordingly.

You will find from time to time in your practice that someone who is not a regular client requests work from you on a "one-time" engagement. This person has a particular need and you are able to provide the service to fill this need. Since he is receiving the benefit of your organization and experience it is entirely in order to make a charge over and above your normal rates for the services rendered. This same principle applies to a client who requires that you drop everything else you are doing to take care of some emergency job that he has. If you respond to this client's need at the inconvenience of yourself and other clients, this should be considered in setting the fee.

Working on a Professional Level

The opportunities for performing work that will bring a premium fee do not come every day. The bulk of the accountant's work will be assignments such as preparation of income tax returns, making an audit of a client's books, preparation of adjusting and closing entries and the like. This work will not bring a premium fee but should bring a professional fee. You cannot expect a professional fee, however, unless you do professional-level work.

Some of the work that small clients request will not be on a professional level. This will likely be in the area of performing write-up work, preparation of payroll records and payroll tax reports, etc. When the accountant is confronted with this problem he must take a hard look at the way in which the work should be organized and accomplished. It should be handled so that he doesn't become "snowed under" with routine clerical-type duties.

Recognize the routine nature of bookkeeping work and try to avoid doing it personally. If you have no staff, of course, you have no choice, but this work should be undertaken only as a temporary measure. The goal should be to relieve yourself of it as soon as possible by employing a staff or having the client's personnel perform the more routine jobs.

This point cannot be stressed too strongly: one of the principal problems in handling small clients will be to get the work and the practice organized so that the work you do personally will be on a professional level. This is the only way you can charge an adequate professional fee for your time.

Types of Fee Arrangements

There are two basic types of fee arrangements:

Per diem rates
Flat or fixed fees

Most accounting firms find that their billings consist of some of both types of fee arrangements. The majority of billings, however, are closely related to actual time expended. Fixed fees are used when the services are of a routine nature, such as bookkeeping services and tax return preparation. The time required to do the work can be accurately predicted and remains relatively constant from year to year. To avoid misunderstandings in fixed fee arrangements, it should be stated clearly by letter that the fixed fee covers certain specified services. Indicate any special or additional services to be billed separately. (See Exhibit 2-1, at the end of this chapter, for such a letter.)

There are indications that fixed fee arrangements are losing favor among accountants and are becoming less widely used. This is due primarily to the problem of constantly increasing costs. The accountant is put in a position of having to absorb these higher costs or having to go back repeatedly to the client requesting an increase in the fee. Many accounting firms are now taking bookkeeping work only on a time basis. They are willing to give the client an estimate of what they think the cost will run, but not willing to agree to a flat monthly fee.

A very good fee arrangement is a monthly retainer against an annual or semi-annual billing. This arrangement has these advantages:

1. Improves cash flow.
2. Gives the client an idea of cost.
3. Avoids a large billing when the work is finished. *Caution—the retainer should be kept in line with changing conditions and cost of living.*

Our firm has been performing write-up work for many years and this part of our practice continues to grow. In the beginning, we agreed to do the client's bookkeeping and income tax work for a flat fee. After a few years, we found it necessary to inform our clients that income tax work would have to be billed separately. It was very difficult to predict the amount of time that would be required to perform income tax service. Some clients raised numerous questions throughout the year regarding the tax implications of certain transactions. Other clients were examined by the Internal Revenue Service. There were too many variations to make it practical to handle income tax work on a fixed fee.

A few years later, we decided that any new bookkeeping clients would be accepted only on a basis of charges for time expended. We have retained fixed fees for existing clients only, and are eliminating these as rapidly as possible. There are two reasons for this. First, the pressures of inflation caused a continuing increase in the cost of performing the service and it was necessary to request fee increases nearly every year. Second, some clients frequently want to discuss various business problems and it is difficult to separate this time from the bookkeeping work. It has been our experience that if a client knows he is going to be charged for all the time expended he will not take up our time unnecessarily.

Records Needed to Assist in Properly Setting Fees

A good billing system requires the accountant to keep good records. Good records help you determine your fee, and are important in case of a dispute over a fee. The vast majority of practitioners are aware of this and have devised systems to fill this need. There are truly a multitude of time-keeping and reporting systems in use in accounting firms around the country. Larger firms are using data processing for their time records. In fact, any practitioner with ten or more employees will find many advantages to a computer processing system. Certain data can be produced concerning chargeable hours, write-downs, etc. that permit the accountant to analyze his operations more effectively.

Any system should be as simple as possible and yet fill the need. The following forms and description cover a simple yet thorough system used by one firm.

The daybook sits on the accountant's desk and is used throughout the day for recording time. The pages are large enough so that a description of the work performed can be written when necessary. Further, it can be used for scheduling appointiments, keeping up with due dates and the like. At billing time, at the end of the month, the accountant can refer back to the day book for descriptive data as to services performed for the client. (See Exhibit 2-2.)

There is some variety among practitioners as to the minimum time breakdown to record. Some record nothing less than a quarter of an hour; others enter tenths of an hour.

Those using the tenth-of-an-hour breakdown feel that the practitioner can do a more effective job of keeping time on telephone calls from clients, questions from staff personnel, etc. Most accountants find that many days are filled with short interruptions, many of which do not justify charging the client for a quarter of an hour.

There are others who will argue that any significant interruption is worth charging the client for a quarter of an hour, and that short interruptions shouldn't be charged. They feel they get a more realistic record of the value of services performed by using the quarter-hour system.

Our firm used the quarter-hour system for many years and then decided to try recording tenths. After experience with both, we prefer the latter.

Sept. 9   19 X4

HOURS	TIME	NAME OF CLIENT	HOURS	TIME	NAME OF CLIENT
8	1 hr.	Firm business	1		4 hours Moore Brothers
9	1 hr.	Smith Ginning Co. Conference re income tax examination	2		work on year-end audit
10	1 hr.	Spradling Hardware review of August financial statement	3		
11	1 hr.	Graham & Co. Conference re need for additional financing	4		↓
	Extra Hours			Extra Hours	

MEMOS & APPOINTMENTS_____

_____

_____

Exhibit 2-2—Daybook Sheets

The time entered in the day book is transferred to the monthly time report where it is totaled and summarized for the month. The report can be prepared, if desired, on a weekly basis at certain times of the year, such as tax season. After the monthly time report has been totaled, the accountant can readily ascertain his total chargeable hours and the potential billing for the month. (See Exhibit 2-3.)

Totals from the monthly time report are posted to individual client ledger sheets. Billing is prepared from the ledger sheet and the accountant is in a position to determine the profit or loss compared with billing rates as he does the billing. Profit or loss figures can be accumulated from month to month through the year. (Exhibit 2-4).

This report enables the acountant to determine how billings for the month compared with standard billing rates and whether the work in progress has increased or decreased. There are certain months in any accounting firm when billings will be unusually high or low. Work in progress will generally increase in a low billing month, or vice versa, and this always should be considered in analyzing the month's results. By considering the change in work in progress, along with the amount of billings, it is possible to determine the actual amount of billable work performed during the month. (See Exhibit 2-5.)

Timing of Billings

Timing is an important consideration in billing. A good rule to follow is to bill as often as possible. There are several reasons for this:

1. The client remembers and appreciates the work performed last month more than the work performed several months ago.
2. Frequent billings help preclude sending a large bill.
3. A number of small bills are generally more acceptable to the client than is one large bill.
4. Frequent billings also help improve the accountant's cash flow and reduce the amount of money tied up in accounts receivable or work in progress.

The timing of billings, of course, has to be acceptable to the client. In many instances, it is not desirable to bill for audit work until the audit has been completed. Further, some clients whose work is primarily tax consultation and preparation of their return prefer to be billed only once a year when the work has been completed. A client's wishes must be respected in these instances. A good rule to bear in mind, however, is that fee arrangements with the client should provide for billings as frequently as possible.

Explaining Fees to Clients

A frank discussion of fees can be helpful. A few years ago, a client complained to me about sending another man to handle some work, instead of doing it

NAME __Richard Wilson__   TIME REPORT

CLIENT'S NAME	ACCT. NO.	TOTALS	DOLLAR COST	28	29	30	31	1	2	3
Johnson Furniture		1	30.00							
River City Co-op		7	210.00			2	3	1		
Jacksonville Pharmacy		6	180.00			1	3	1		
Valley News Service		5	150.00			1			4	
Peters & Son		8	240.00							
Moore Brothers		14	420.00							1
Smith Corporation		8	240.00						2	1
Spradling Hardware		7	210.00							2
Graham & Co.		6	180.00							
Dr. H. L. Jones		6	180.00							
Suburban Casuals		18	540.00							
Twin City Music		7	210.00							
Forest Nursery		8	240.00							
Estate of Alfred Young		24	720.00							
FIRM		27	810				4		2	
PROFESSIONAL DEVEL. COURSE		8	240							
TOTAL		160	4800				8		8	8

List expenses chargeable to client on reverse side of this report.

Exhibit 2-3—Monthly Time Report

MONTH _SEPTEMBER, 19X4_

4	5	6	7	8	9	10	11	12	13	14	15	16	17	18	19	20	21	22	23	24	25	26	27
				1																			
				1																			
							1																
			8																				
3					4								6										
4					1																		
				2	1								2										
					1		3				2												
										3	1							2					
										3	3	8		2				2					
														4					3				
																	7	1					
																			8	8	8		
4	1				4	1		4		2	2			2			1						
							8																
8	8			8	8	8	8	8		8	8	8	8	8			8	8	8	8	8		

Exhibit 2-3—Monthly Time Report (continued)

SWANSONS MANS SHOP

(1) DATE	(2) NAME	(3) TIME	(4) EXPENSES	(5)	(6) TOTAL COST	(7) INVOICE No.	(8) DR.	(9) CR.	(10) BALANCE	(11) PROFIT (LOSS) CURRENT MONTH	(12) PROFIT (LOSS) YEAR TO DATE
APR. 5-13 MAY	LG BR MA	20 44 6	Postage	50	6950	445	7150	750	0	7	4
6-11 JUNE	BR MA	38 5			43	790	4700	4700	0	7	(1)
7-13 JULY	BR MA	45 10			44	7000	7000	0		(77)	(1)
	LG BR MA	20 44 5			67		7000			3	2

Prepared By ____ Initials ____ Date ____
Approved By ____

Exhibit 2-4—Client Ledger Sheet

	Work in progress, Sept. 1	September charges	September billings	Profit (loss)	Work in progress, Sept. 30
Johnson Furniture	10000	3000			13000
River City Co-op	5000	21000	27000	1000	-0-
Jacksonville Pharmacy	7500	18000	25000	< 500 >	-0-
Valley News Service	10000	15000			25000
Peters & Son	-0-	24000	25000	1000	-0-
Moore Brothers	-0-	45000	20000	-0-	25000
Smith Corporation	-0-	24000			24000
Spradling Hardware	10000	21000	30000	< 1000 >	-0-
Graham & Co.	-0-	18000			18000
Dr. H. L. Jones	5000	18000	25000	2000	-0-
Suburban Casuals	-0-	54000	55000	1000	-0-
Twin City Music	6000	21000			27000
Forest Nursery	20000	24000	45000	1000	-0-
Estate of Alfred Young	10000	74000	84500	500	-0-
	83500	375000	334500	5000	179000

Exhibit 2-5—Monthly Analysis of Billing and Work in Progress

myself. It turned out that the client thought we charged the same rates for all accountants in the firm. As a result, we discussed fees in one of our client bulletins. (See Exhibit 2-6 at the end of this chapter.)

Collecting the Fee

One of the unfortunate facts of life for accountants is that not all clients pay their fees promptly. A collection effort by the accountant, even though distasteful, is necessary from time to time.

Some practitioners feel it destroys their relationship with the client to push personally for collection of delinquent fees. There are ways to work around their problem. Some firms review their list of delinquent accounts around the 20th of the month and have the secretary make a reminder telephone call to selected clients. A polite reminder from the secretary that the account is past due, with a request for a check, can be effective. The secretary should be instructed to be pleasant and never to argue with the client. This is an impersonal approach and does not involve the accountant himself.

There are times when it is effective to send a collection letter which is impersonal in tone, such as that in Exhibit 2-7. While a written request for payment is not generally as effective as personal contact, a letter phrased in this manner will often get the client's attention and cause him to make payment.

One system that is used by some firms in dealing with seriously delinquent clients is to obtain a note from the client which is sold by the accountant to his bank. The principal advantage of this is that it puts the client in a position of having to make payment to the bank. Experience has clearly shown that most people will pay a note to a bank more promptly than they will pay other debts. The client, therefore, can be expected to make prompt payment to the bank when the note becomes due whereas he might "ride" the accountant for a longer period of time.

Conclusion

It takes more than technical competence to be a successful accountant. It takes ability to manage your practice. It takes the know-how and determination to charge an adequate professional fee.

Your clients want to feel that they have an accountant who is successful in his field. Success is an indication that the professional man knows his business. Further, there is an element of prestige involved in using the "best" accounting firm, and most clients enjoy prestige.

All this is to say that the economic well being of your practice is extremely important. Knowing when and how to bill, when to charge a premium fee, how to keep proper time records is vital.

Always keep in mind that the client needs your services, and therefore, can afford to pay for them. It's up to you to convince him of your value!

Dear Mr. Wagner:

This letter is written to outline the nature of the services we will be performing for you and the financial arrangements for the work.

Our work will generally consist of performing the following services for you:

1. We will perform bookkeeping services consisting of preparation of journals, ledgers, employee earning records and the like that will be used in preparing financial statements and tax returns.
2. We will prepare financial statements monthly.
3. We will prepare quarterly payroll tax, sales tax and occupancy tax reports.
4. We will provide you with information regarding your business to be used in the preparation of your personal income tax return and will prepare your return, if you wish.

The financial statements will be prepared without audit and will be marked "unaudited". The work we will be performing will be accounting service and not audit service, and we will not express an auditor's opinion on the financial statements. Our work is not designed to disclose defalcations or irregularities in your operation, although their discovery may result.

Our fee for this service will be $200.00 per month. We will strive to perform this work for the agreed fee as long as possible, but may find it necessary to request an adjustment in the future if the amount of work changes or if our costs increase.

The monthly fee will include a reasonable amount of time for review and discussion of the financial statements. Income tax service, including preparation of income tax returns, tax examinations and tax planning will be billed separately. We will also bill separately for any special services requiring a significant amount of time.

You may be assured that your affairs will have our most careful attention and that it is our aim to give you the best service possible.

Very truly yours,

Exhibit 2-1—Letter Relative to Fixed Fee Arrangement

LONG, CHILTON & COMPANY
CLIENT BULLETIN

The subject of accounting fees is obviously of interest both to us and to our clients. You as a client want to feel you are getting your money's worth for the fee you pay, and we must have fees that are adequate to enable us to give good service. This bulletin, therefore, will endeavor to explain some of the things that enter into the determination of our fees.

Many of the other professions have "fee schedules", which provide for a certain fee for a specific service, such as performing a surgical operation or designing a new building. Many people think accountants have a fee schedule covering audits and preparation of tax returns. This is not practical and is not a common practice among CPA's. Each audit and each tax return is different and therefore must be charged for individually.

The most common method of determining fees for accounting work is based on the time involved. This method has been found to be the fairest for all concerned, and is used extensively by most CPA's, including our firm. Other factors can sometimes enter into the picture, however. Some of these are discussed below.

First, with a staff of some twenty five people, we have individuals with various levels of training and experience. The billing rates of these individuals varies considerably. We feel that in order to arrive at a fair fee we must assign a person at the right level of experience. We can't expect a client to pay $20.00 per hour for a job that should be done for $10.00. This is one reason you frequently find the partners assigning work to others.

Second, when charging by the hour, we have to do an efficient job to justify the charge. If we take 20 hours to do a job that should take 10, we do not feel justified in charging our regular rate. On the other hand, if we are able to perform a valuable service for you in a minimum of time due to prior experience, we may feel justified in charging a higher rate. Superior performance justifies a higher fee, poor performance necessitates a lower fee.

In much of the work we do, we are able to reasonably predict how much time it should take and are willing to make an estimate of the fee in advance. We realize that clients generally want some idea of the cost they will incur. Such estimates cannot be "firm" figures, since we cannot always predict just what we will run into in a job. Our profession prohibits us from bidding against other CPA's for work. Price competition generally results in lowering the quality of accounting services and in the long run hurts the client.

The major factor affecting accounting fees today is the cost of getting, training and keeping a good staff. Without a good staff we cannot render service. To get good people we must pay competitive salaries and the current trend in salaries is definitely upward.

Over the years our clients have raised few questions with us about our fees. We hope you have felt that you have been getting your money's worth with us. This discussion should help you gain an understanding of this subject from our standpoint.

Exhibit 2-6—Client Bulletin Regarding Fees

Mr. Randolph Johnson
Brownsville, Texas

Dear Mr. Johnson:

Upon reviewing our accounts receivable we find that your account is
one that is considerably past due. Past due accounts receivable are
quite a problem for us at the present time and we ask that you give us
a payment on your account.

It might appear that a firm such as ours rendering a service rather
than selling merchandise would not need to press for collections. We
have the same expenses as any other business, however, including a
sizable payroll, and cannot carry accounts receivable for a long period
of time.

Please let us have your check without further delay.

                                        Very truly yours,

Exhibit 2-7—Collection Letter Written in an Impersonal Tone

CHAPTER 3

Being Responsive to the Small Client's Needs

You are working in your office on a quiet Tuesday morning when small client Walter Mathers drops by to discuss a notice he has received from the Internal Revenue Service. After disposing of the IRS notice, you chat for a few minutes and Walter is about to leave. At the door, he turns and comments, "By the way, I have been looking at that motel property at the edge of town that was foreclosed on a couple of months ago. I believe I can buy it and profitably convert it into apartments."

It is quickly apparent to you that making such a move would be a major undertaking for Walter. He is a successful merchant but it would be necessary for him to borrow substantially to purchase this property and remodel it. You make some inquiries as to the asking price of the property and what the remodeling cost would run. Walter says that he has talked to a contractor or two who advised him that it would be very difficult to give an estimate without plans or specifications. He feels that it might be necessary to have the remodeling work done on a cost plus basis.

At this point, you suggest that Walter come back in and sit down so this can be discussed more fully. You point out that it is quite important to know not only the capital expenditure he will have involved in this venture, but that there are substantial operating expenses that should be considered. You suggest that Walter consider hiring an architect or at least talk again to the contractors, and that in the meantime you will assemble some operating costs on an annual basis. Walter agrees.

You spend some time in the next two or three days contacting the local tax authorities, insurance men and others to obtain some of the figures. You also review files of other clients operating apartments or motels in order to determine all the various expenses that will be incurred, and make estimates of utilities, maintenance, supplies and the like.

Another meeting is held with Walter and the projected annual operating expenses are reviewed. He has not even considered that some of the expenses will be necessary and it becomes apparent that there will be a cash deficit of several thousand dollars per year. Walter is in a position to invest such an amount into the venture to keep it solvent, but will now have to decide whether or not he wants to do so. The picture you have given him is considerably different from what he was anticipating earlier. Now he has a much more realistic outlook on the project.

As Walter leaves, he expresses his appreciation for the work you have done and comments that he is certainly happy that he mentioned this to you before he had gotten into the project any deeper.

This is not a particularly unusual situation and the services rendered in this case are those any client should expect from his accountant. The significant point is, however, that when the client mentioned what he was thinking about the accountant was alert and recognized that the client needed some help. He picked up the ball and ran with it, suggesting what he thought should be done. This accountant was indeed responsive to the needs of the client.

Maintaining the Personal Touch

To be responsive to the needs of this client, the practitioner must be familiar with the client's affairs. Keep in touch—maintain personal contact. As the practice grows, this becomes a bigger problem. How can you have a growing practice and still retain a personal touch with each client?

One rule to keep in mind is that once you have obtained a good working knowledge of the client's affairs, it is easier to keep up with them. When a new client comes in, the accountant should spend enough personal time to obtain a thorough understanding of his business. There are many experienced accountants who have not actually worked on the books of a particular client for many years, but who still have a good working knowledge of the client's affairs. This is due to the fact that they set up the books at the beginning and this knowledge has stayed with them through the years.

It requires initiative to keep up with the client and his problems. If you have a client from whom you have heard nothing in two or three months, it is advisable to invite him to lunch or to drop by his business for a visit. Such a visit should simply be for the purpose of finding out how things are going in his business. The client will be pleased at the interest you have shown and will often get into a significant discussion of business problems. The discussion will, as often as not, result in some additional work for the accountant. This is client relations at its best—the ingredient that builds a practice.

Maintaining a Fresh Viewpoint

Most clients continue to employ the same accountant year after year and never seriously consider changing. The practitioner has a responsibility to keep alert and maintain a fresh reaction to the client's affairs. Working with the same financial statements, same audits, same procedures year after year tends to have a hypnotic effect and causes the accountant to lose the fresh viewpoint.

When a new client is first obtained, the practitioner has his best opportunity to get a fresh reaction to the client's accounting system and business operations. This reaction should be put on paper immediately and can prove to be a valuable reference in the future. If the client's office procedures or accounting system leave something to be desired, the first impression will usually show this. After the accountant has handled the account for a number of years, he may have become accustomed to the poor procedures and lost his perspective in dealing with them.

There are certain techniques to be used in maintaining the fresh viewpoint after several years of dealing with the client. Personnel should be rotated at reasonable intervals if at all possible. Always look for better ways to do the job, short cuts and time-saving techniques. How about his financial statements? For how many years have they been prepared in the same format? Perhaps some new statistics would be helpful. An annual look at his tax situation for planning possibilities is a must. Does he need better overall financial planning through the use of a budget? Are changes being made each year in audit programs?

You are close to your clients and their businesses. You probably have been so for many years, hence the need to stay alert and keep a fresh outlook. But remember this: the client is a lot closer to the business than you are. He is running it every day, all day. He is the one who may not be able to see the forest for the trees. He needs the fresh approach, too, and that's your job. Keep your viewpoint fresh so you can help the client with his.

Train your staff to be alert to any change in the client's affairs and to report this information. Alertness on the part of the staff can be an invaluable help. Some firms have even developed questionnaires or forms to be used for this purpose (See Exhibit 3-1.) Regardless of the procedure used, it should be emphasized that feedback of any information obtained about the client helps the firm to serve him better.

Providing the Client with a Sounding Board

One of the biggest needs served by most accountants is that of providing a sounding board for the small client. These people, in most cases, have no one with whom they can discuss their business affairs. Many times they have no board of directors or partners. They may have reservations about discussing all their problems with their banker. They simply need someone to talk to. The accountant should be willing to take the time to talk and, above all, be able to discuss the client's business intelligently. Some practitioners give the impression that they are interested primarily in the figures, books and financial statements and are not interested in, or qualified to, discuss the operating problems of the business. This is a regrettable situation. It deprives the accountant of an opportunity to be of service and deprives the client of valuable assistance.

In our firm we have tried to serve as counselors to our clients. If one is building a new plant or developing a subdivision and wants us to look it over, we do. If he wants to discuss the pros and cons of going into a new venture or developing a new product, we help him all we can. If he wants assistance in buying out a partner, or bringing in a new one, we respond. Trying to help clients with the diverse problems that come up can take the accountant far afield from conventional accounting, but this should be looked on as an interesting challenge.

A Quick Response with Information

A responsive accountant learns to know when his client needs certain information quickly and arranges to meet this need promptly. Such a situation recently happened to one firm in a case of a motel client. Write-up work was being performed for the motel, with monthly financial statements issued between the 15th and 20th of each month. During the heavy tourist season the statement for June, which was issued around July 15th, indicated that cost of food sold in the motel restaurant was considerably higher than it should have been. In the discussion with the client it was pointed out that this information was coming to him rather late, since half of July had already gone by without any corrective action being taken. It was decided, therefore, that another food inventory would be taken as of July 20 and the gross profit calculated immediately for the first 20 days of July. The accountant sent a member of his staff to the motel to assist in getting the figures together for this special report, which was available on July 22. As a result of this prompt report, steps were taken to correct certain practices in the kitchen, and food cost again came in line.

Clients are especially appreciative of receiving information they need without waiting for the full typed report to be prepared. The accountant who will pick up the telephone and give his client certain figures early is doing a valuable service. Accountants have been justifiably criticized for making the client wait for needed information while the books are brought into balance and the figures typed. In many instances, the client is more interested in getting the figures he needs at an early date than he is in having everything adjusted to the penny and the report typed. Learn to detect when your client wants this early information and make arrangements to provide it for him.

Learn to Deal with People

An accounting practice is essentially a matter of dealing with people and their problems. These problems, of course, fall into the fields of income tax, accounting, auditing and financial matters. The successful accountant must know his business in these areas. To achieve full success, however, he also must master the art of dealing with people. A public accountant deals with a wide range of people and must truly enjoy helping them with their problems. He must be a close observer of human nature and learn all he can about his clients. His judgment of human nature should enable him to have a good idea of what makes the client tick.

If we accountants were to describe the ideal client, we would probably come up with a man who is aggressive, ambitious, knows how to plan and organize, how to get along with people, how to handle money, who is looking to the future, who is demanding and yet reasonable to work with, who can communicate, and most important of all, who knows how to use, and appreciates the value of, professional services.

Unfortunately, the vast majority of clients do not measure up to this description. Most of the people with whom we deal have various failings (as do their accountants). We have to deal with them as we find them and make the best of it. But this is part of the challenge of our profession. It requires us to work at the job of developing techniques for dealing with various types of people. Here are a few typical clients that we all encounter.

The Client with Drive and Ambition

The client with drive and ambition who is trying to expand his business is, in many respects, the best client an accountant can have. His expansion policies can provide an ever increasing need for our services. He will be bringing up new and different problems all the time. On the other hand, he may take action and make decisions about which you know nothing until later. He may be demanding and require a great deal from you. He should be educated to discuss his plans before he takes action. You will occasionally need to advise him against making a certain move. Such advice should be given constructively with your reasons clearly expressed. Don't give the impression of being a conservative accountant who is opposed to progress. Let him know you are interested in helping him expand. At the same time, let him understand he can expect honest advice that may not always agree with his own ideas.

The Client Who Can't Handle Money

The world is full of people who can't handle money. Every accountant will acquire one or more of them as clients. They probably come to you initially for tax advice, but also need financial advice. There is a great opportunity to help the client if he is willing to listen.

In some instances, you will be dealing with a business man who is able to operate successfully over a period of time—but sooner or later will make the wrong move. He may decide to expand at the wrong time. He may be in a business that has major fluctuations, but refuses to cut back on overhead while waiting for business to pick up.

There are no hard and fast rules for advising such clients. Some need to be taught to look before they leap—to make a careful study before reaching major decisions. Others have to be encouraged to get behind the day-to-day operations of their business or to stop procrastinating on tough decisions. It takes skill and finesse to deal with these diverse individuals, and perhaps some help from the client's lawyer or banker.

Many salaried clients or professional men develop a good income but can't hold onto their money due to poor investments or excessive personal expenditures. Some accountants have worked with such clients in setting up personal budgets or even in assisting them in handling their funds. While it may be rather expensive for the individual to pay his accountant to perform this service, it should be looked upon as an investment that will pay dividends in the long run. A relationship of this type need not continue indefinitely, but is an educational process which will terminate after the client has learned to handle his own finances.

The Client Who Can't Quite Succeed

Some clients are talented in a particular field, such as selling, but do not have overall business and administrative ability to succeed on their own. We have had clients who did a great job of planning, but could not effectively put the plans into operation. In many instances, such clients can be trained to become better administrators or financial managers. On the other hand, there are those who would be better off working for someone else. They struggle along for years without ever achieving any real success. It sometimes reaches a point where you may feel you owe it to the client to suggest that he consider selling out. This is difficult advice to give, but is badly needed in some situations.

The Client Who Won't Take Your Advice

You can't do business for long with a client who shows a flagrant disregard for your advice, especially in basic accounting and tax matters. It is not so bad if he asks your opinion on general business problems and does otherwise. But in accounting and tax matters, you are the expert and should expect your advice to be followed the majority of the time. If not, the client presumably has no confidence in you and you would both be better off with a change.

Some clients have to be shown that you mean business. This can be done by a frank discussion or, in some cases, more appropriately by a letter. Some years ago we acquired a client who was already in trouble with the Internal Revenue Service due to woefully inadequate records. He was under an examination which was not going well. We told him what had to be done to settle the examination and how to keep out of trouble in the future.

He found this advice hard to take and argued and complained at great length. The relationship became frustrating. We were also concerned because we had done a considerable amount of work without sending a bill. It was decided that we should bring the matter to a head by sending a bill at premium rates for the work done to date, accompanied by a strong letter telling him what had to be done. A sample of such a letter is found in Exhibit 3-2.

This letter got the client's attention. He calmed down, paid the bill and started taking our advice more seriously. Another client, of course, could have taken the other obvious course and changed accountants. In either case, we would have been better off. Don't struggle along with a client who doesn't respect your advice.

How to Part Company with a Client

Several years ago, our firm received a letter from an important client advising that they were changing accountants. The annual audit had recently been completed. It had taken a great deal of time, relations had become strained and the fee had been high. We felt that most of the fault was with the client's office manager, but the client obviously had been convinced that we were at fault.

We felt we didn't deserve to lose this client, and were tempted to let him know in no uncertain terms how we felt. Fortunately, better judgment prevailed. We wrote a letter expressing our regret at losing the account, offering to do anything possible to assist their new accountants and wishing the best of luck in the future. An example of such a letter is found in Exhibit 3-3.

A few weeks later, one of our partners ran into the client, who commented that he had now decided that some of his problems were with the office manager. Not long after that, we heard the office manager had been fired. Within a few days, the client asked us to send a man out to help bring the books up to date. We are still working for this client today.

Not every case of a lost client turns out as happily as this one. There was a bit of luck involved in this case, but one point can be made; if we had given vent to our frustrations at the time, we would never have gotten the client back. We made the break like gentlemen, and our final impression was a good one.

When you lose a client, leave in as friendly a manner as possible. If he leaves with good feelings toward you, he may someday return. At least, he is less likely to tell all his acquaintances about his problems with you. A former client usually is dissatisfied with your work. If he is also unfriendly, he can damage your reputation. Even though he is dissatisfied, at least try to part company on friendly terms.

Conclusion

A public accountant needs to become adept at human relations. An important phase of your work involves dealing with people. Maintain a personal touch with all of your clients, keep a fresh viewpoint on their problems and come up with a timely and appropriate response to their needs. This requires the ability to be sensitive to others and to adjust to changing problems.

1   Indicate significant personnel changes.

2. Any changes in geographical areas served?   Opening or closing of branch
    offices or stores?

3. Any changes in methods of selling?

4. Any changes in products or services offered?

5. Any changes in capital structure?

6. Indicate significant changes in financial position and the reasons therefore

7. Has the client changed banks or attorneys?

8. Any changes in ownership?

Exhibit 3-1—Annual Report on Changes in Client Affairs

Mr. Samuel Brown
National Industries
Brownsville, Texas

Dear Mr. Brown:

We are enclosing our bill for services rendered to date in connection with your income tax examination. This bill is based on the time required to handle this work up to this point as well as the complexities involved.

We have been trying to get a better understanding of your operations and some of the transactions under examination, but are frankly having a difficult time. To be blunt, your accounting records leave a lot to be desired. It is not surprising that the Revenue Agent is suspicious that you are not reporting all your income. All these problems have been brought on by your failure to accept the fact that adequate records must be maintained.

In order to properly serve you we are going to have to have all the facts. You must have enough confidence in us to give us the complete story. As an example, we cannot have bank accounts suddenly appear without a previous record showing the source of the money that went into this account. The Revenue Agent will invariably pick this up as unreported income.

We will appreciate receiving your check in payment of the enclosed invoice, and ask that you give me a call at an early date so we can discuss some of the problems pertaining to the examination.

                              Very truly yours,

Exhibit 3-2—Strong Letter to a Client Who Won't Take Advice

Mr. John Jones
Delta Supply Company
Brownsville, Texas

Dear Mr. Jones:

This will acknowledge with regret your recent letter in which you advise that
you have decided to change accounting firms.

We recognize the many problems you and your people have had in recent months.
We know that your accounting personnel have put in long hours in an effort to
overcome some of these problems.

From our standpoint the difficulties encountered in performing the audit just
recently completed have been quite distressing to us. It would serve no useful purpose at this late date to review these difficulties or the reasons for
them. Let me simply say that we worked very hard to give you a professional
job.

Your letter indicates that your decision is final. We accept this decision
reluctantly, and assure you that we wish nothing but the best to you and your
organization. We will certainly cooperate in every manner possible with you
and your new auditors.

                              Very truly yours,

Exhibit 3-3—Letter, to Client Who Is Changing to Another Accountant

CHAPTER **4**

Developing Effective Communications with the Small Client

Accountants usually communicate by means of speaking, observing and listening, writing and reading. Material can be sent and received in an endless variety of ways, such as financial statements, charts, graphs, movies, tape cassettes, lectures, discussions, and so on.

Effective Communications: Opening Channels to Bigger Profits

Studies have revealed that well over 50 percent of the time of professional men is spent in communicating. If you think about your activities during the day, it is difficult to discover much time when you are not engaged in some form of communication. You are in contact most frequently with clients and staff associates, but also with Revenue Agents, bankers, lawyers and a multitude of others.

The effectiveness of your professional work will inevitably be linked directly to the effectiveness of your communications.

Setting Objectives in Communicating

When engaged in communication, the accountant is attempting to convey or to receive useful knowledge or ideas. Fees are generated by selling useful knowledge and ideas to clients. The ability to convey this information is obviously important. But don't forget that you have to acquire this knowledge before you can sell it. So the receiving end of the communications is equally important.

The accountant should keep the word "useful" clearly in mind. Clients are noticeably lukewarm about paying for a report which offers no useful material.

Further, the client has the privilege of judging what is useful. A neat, perfectly balanced financial statement is not useful if the client does not understand it. Accountants deal in a technical, complex field and have to make their product useful to the layman.

When you communicate effectively and convey useful information you are selling yourself to the client. This is a by-product of good communication, and a not insignificant one. Selling yourself is the principal factor in building a practice. Nothing helps more than effective, useful communication.

Effective Speaking

When communicating orally you are "on stage." The listener is watching your every action and expression. Here are some of the ingredients of effective speaking: self confidence; a clear, easily understood speaking voice; knowing when to change voice tone or inflection to highlight a point; skillful use of the hands and facial expression. You are an expert speaking to laymen, and the importance of self-confidence cannot be over-emphasized.

Many people tend to rush their speech when they are under pressure or pushed for time. Accountants are frequently subject to these problems and should be on the alert for rapid delivery. You especially need to speak effectively at such a time and use all your speaking skills.

Effective Listening

Becoming an effective listener is often more of a problem than becoming a good speaker. The reason: most of us enjoy talking more than we do listening. We tend to be impatient when it comes our turn to listen. Many opportunities for effective communication are lost, or at least partially lost, by failure to listen properly.

Listening requires concentration. Look the speaker in the eye and let him know you are interested. Be alert for changes in facial expression or tone of voice that can give additional insight into the speaker's words. Think about what he is saying (and not saying). Be thinking of questions that will facilitate the discussion.

One area where the accountant should be especially adept as a listener is in interviewing clients for tax return preparation. This is a situation where it is easy to miss some important information. The client does not know the many factors affecting his return and the accountant occasionally fails to ask all the necessary questions. Often, the client will mention something during the interview which will provide a lead regarding an item that could have been overlooked. This is one area and only one of many—where proper listening habits will enable the accountant to do a better job.

Effective Writing

Written communication may not take as much of your time as the spoken word but it is fully as important. Your work requires regular writing; letters, reports, memoranda and the like. Important advice should be given in writing. Learn to evaluate your writing critically. Do not use any more words than necessary. Excess wordage clutters up the message and detracts from what you are saying. Make your sentences short. Use words that move the message along. Your readers are busy men and have more to read than time permits. Develop your writing so that when your clients receive a communication from you it will be to the point, interesting and useful.

Effective Reading

Accountants can agree on this: the reading material coming across their desks keeps increasing year by year. One accountant who has been in practice many years estimates that he has two to four times the material to read that he had 20 years ago. This is a typical situation. How do you cope with this problem?

Certainly no one can read everything that is available. It is necessary to be selective in choosing reading material. The reader must concentrate on what is most important. For the tax practitioner, keeping up to date with the continual changes is a must. Here, again, be selective in the tax material you read.

It is a mistake, however, to restrict your reading solely to accounting and business publications. To become a well-rounded individual it is necessary to read widely. This brings knowledge concerning the world about you. Keep up with current events and books that are of interest. Reading in unrelated fields gives a broad perspective and keeps the mind alert.

To do this it is necessary to read rapidly. It is said that President Kennedy could read 1,200 words per minute—a phenomenal rate of speed. Check your reading speed. If it is under 300 words per minute you should strive to improve it.

One method of covering more territory when reading is to know when to scan. At times you will simply be trying to get the main idea or looking for one particular point. Scanning rather than careful reading is often appropriate.

It is a big challenge to make the most valuable use of our time. Improving your reading skills is one way to do it.

Special Ways of Communicating

Most communication with clients is through established methods: audit reports, letters, financial statements, memoranda, etc. Let us assume you have developed your skills in each of these areas. Now you are looking for new and different ways to communicate. What are some of these?

Client Newsletter– Some firms have developed the practice of sending a regular newsletter to clients on subjects of interest. These usually are one page in length and are generally issued once a month. The topics covered are those on which the accountant can speak with authority. They should be selected so that the client is made aware of the range of professional skills of his accountant. Articles can be written on accounting, income tax, estate planning, management counseling and the like. It is also wise to keep the client advised about the growth of the firm, as well as mentioning honors received or speeches made by partners and staff.

Our firm has used a client newsletter for a number of years and the results have been quite satisfactory. We do not establish a rigid schedule but try to get one out monthly if possible. In actual practice, eight to ten newsletters are issued each year. Income tax subjects are emphasized more strongly during the late fall and winter months. During the spring and summer, management services, estate planning and various other topics are covered. Usually, each newsletter will bring a handful of comments or inquiries from clients. We get enough client reaction to give us the incentive to keep the newsletters coming. A sample is presented in Exhibit 4-1.

Sending Pertinent Material to Clients–When reading the latest bulletin from your income tax service, you may notice that a bill has been introduced in Congress that will directly affect one of your clients. Make a copy of this material and send it to him. The same can be done with clippings from *The Wall Street Journal* and other business publications.

This keeps the client informed as well as letting him know you are thinking of his problems. If you are alert, you will run into a surprising number of items that can be sent to clients. This is not only good client relations, it is good service. It may help him avoid a problem or take advantage of an opportunity.

Developing Special Client Reports–One of the best methods for helping the small client is to create special financial data that he needs. This data may fall outside the conventional financial statements and may be provided on a daily basis. Many small business men have difficulty obtaining current operating data when they need it. Use of some imagination and effort on your part can help overcome this problem.

Nearly any business could benefit from some form of daily report which highlights the day's business operations. It can be extremely important to management if it is timely and simplified so that it can be reviewed quickly each day. Such a report should cover those items of the company's operations which are the very heartbeat of the business. It should give the principal operating figures for the day as well as cash position, accounts receivable, orders received, production data, and the like. Examples of two typical reports are in Exhibits 4-2 and 4-3.

A cash projection is another very useful special report. Many clients have difficulty in anticipating the ups and downs of cash flow, and run into unexpected difficulty. The accountant can analyze cash flow trends and prepare monthly or quarterly cash flow projections. This report should be in the format most useful to the client, but should tell him when he will run short of cash and have to borrow money.

Communicating about the Financial Statement

You have completed your year-end financial statement of Central Food Distributors and are getting ready to prepare your comments prior to meeting with the client. You feel you have done a good job on the books. As you begin to collect your thoughts about reporting to the client, it occurs to you that in many respects this is the most important part of the assignment. Even though you have prepared a good financial statement, the client will have little appreciation of this unless you are able to provide him with useful knowledge and ideas.

You realize that the client has limited knowledge of financial statements. He has indicated that he feels that you are the expert and should give him the answers he needs. He does not understand all the terms an accountant uses, is not clear on how certain figures are determined and may not take the time to review the report as thoroughly as you have.

In preparing the report, try to place yourself in the client's position. What information does he want? Here are some points about which you should be prepared to communicate.

Interpreting the Operating Results—In presenting earnings, give the client some yardsticks with which to judge the figures. Show the operating results for the current year compared with the preceding year. Compare earnings with the budget (if they have one) and with any reliable industry statistics you can obtain. Give your opinion on the adequacy of the earnings and any trends that you note in the operating results.

What happened to the money?—Next, head off the question of what became of the money. Clients who are earning good profits on which they are having to pay income tax always want to know what happened to the money. A condensed summary showing sources and application of working capital will give this information.

The client will want to know everything you can tell him about the condition of his assets and liabilities, so you should show him the aging of accounts receivable, inventory, accounts payable and the like, indicating favorable or unfavorable trends that you detect.

Try to look to the future, indicating to the client his commitments for the coming year such as retirement of long-term debt and additions to plant and equipment. Indicate his need for X dollars to meet these commitments, either through earnings or borrowing.

Reporting to the Client—Write your report so that this information is covered in a clear and understandable manner. In this way, both the client and others who read it will have a clear picture of the status and progress of the company. Plan to meet with the client and discuss your findings and conclusions in as much detail as necessary. If you are meeting with a board of directors, review the report page by page, pointing out significant items and answering questions. You may need to work up some summaries of pertinent points or to prepare graphs to use in the meeting.

If you present reports to your clients in this manner, you are doing a good job of communicating. You are putting proper emphasis on this important area and are avoiding the temptation to become so involved in the figures that you fail to consider what they meant to the client.

Exhibits 4-4 and 4-5 present two examples of the types of communication described above. Exhibit 4-4 is a report on an audit, whereas Exhibit 4-5 is a presentation of an unaudited financial statement. In both cases, a full explanation of the financial picture has been presented.

This point should be emphasized: you can't be a successful accountant unless you can communicate. All the technical competence in the world will not get the job done by itself; it must be linked to an ability to make your product useful to the client. Tell your story so that the client understands it. Speak and listen effectively and well, and you will be a more successful accountant.

Use of Charts—The old adage that "a picture is worth a thousand words" should be borne in mind. Most people become easily discouraged when trying to understand a page full of figures. In many instances, the message can be communicated more effectively by use of a chart. In Exhibit 4-6, there is a chart highlighting certain important figures taken from the report of Triangle Processing Company. The client may get a clearer understanding of the trends from that chart than he can from either the financial statements or the accountant's comments.

The accountant does not have to be an accomplished artist to prepare such charts. They need not be included in the typed report itself, but can be handed to the client as a separate exhibit when reviewing the report with him.

LONG, CHILTON, PAYTE & HARDIN

CLIENT BULLETIN

We recently ran across the following article describing why an accountant is uniquely qualified to assist his client in estate planning. Here are some of the points covered:

> The accountant is well versed in income tax matters and an important element of estate planning involves a consideration of income tax consequences.

> He is familiar with the financial affairs of his client. Often he is in an excellent position to figure out net worth, project earnings and compile other information with a minimum of effort. This is important because effective estate planning must be founded on accurate current data and on reliable future expectations.

> Due to his constant contact with the client, the accountant is in a position to spot problems. On the one hand, he knows when the client has reached a financial level to make estate planning feasible. Also he is best able to detect changes in the client's financial status which may necessitate modification of existing estate plans.

> Many accountants, through training, are capable of exercising a great deal of independent judgment. This could be indispensable in evaluating insurance program, the funding of buy and sell agreements, investment counseling, and other arrangements.

> The relationship between the client and the accountant is usually a continuing one extending over a period of years. This enables him to watch for changes in the law and in the client's financial affairs which may necessitate revisions in the estate plan. He frequently knows the client and his family well enough to be aware of their long range objectives.

Estate planning normally involves a team effort consisting of the accountant, attorney, bank trust officer and life insurance underwriter. We work with these other professionals in the field but frequently initiate estate planning because of our frequent contact with our clients.

Most people prefer to ignore estate planning. If you are past 45 years of age, you should know the answers to the following questions:

> How much am I worth at this time?
> What would be the size of my estate, considering life insurance proceeds?
> What would it cost to pay estate taxes and administration costs?

Exhibit 4-1—Client Bulletin

SULLIVAN AND COMPANY
DAILY MANAGEMENT REPORT
DATE_____

CASH

Cash on deposit, beginning	$_____
Deposits today	
Checks today	(_____)
Cash on deposit, ending	$_____

RECEIVABLES

Accounts receivable, beginning	$_____
Sales today	
Collections on account today	(_____)
Accounts receivable, ending	$_____

PAYABLES

Accounts payable, beginning	$_____
Invoices received today	
Payments made today	(_____)
Accounts payable, ending	$_____

PURCHASE COMMITMENTS

Purchased orders outstanding, beginning	$_____
PO's issued today	
PO's filled today	
Purchase orders outstanding	$_____

Other items that could be covered:
   Sales - analyzed by salesman, by territory, by product as to cash and charge.
   Overtime - hours worked, overtime pay.
   Production - by units, by product.

Any of these statistics could be compared with those of previous periods.

Exhibit 4-2—Sample Special Client Report

BIG CIRCLE INDUSTRIES, INC.

WEEKLY ACTIVITY REPORT

WEEK ENDING JUNE 30, 19__

JOBS IN PROCESS AT END OF WEEK:

JOB NO.	TOTAL COST TO DATE
_____	_____
_____	_____
_____	_____
_____	_____
_____	_____
_____	_____
_____	_____
_____	_____
_____	_____
_____	_____
TOTAL	$ _____

JOBS COMPLETED AND BILLED DURING WEEK:

JOB NO.	AMOUNT BILLED	COST OF JOB
_____	_____	_____
_____	_____	_____
_____	_____	_____
_____	_____	_____
_____	_____	_____
_____	_____	_____
_____	_____	_____
_____	_____	_____

TOTAL JOBS COMPLETED
    THIS MONTH   _____   _____

TOTAL JOBS COMPLETED
    THIS YEAR   _____   _____

CASH IN BANK AT END OF WEEK $ _____

ACCOUNTS RECEIVABLE AT END OF WEEK $ _____

ACCOUNTS PAYABLE AT END OF WEEK   _____

Exhibit 4-3—Weekly Activity Report

MEMBERS AMERICAN INSTITUTE OF CERTIFIED PUBLIC ACCOUNTANTS

LONG, CHILTON & COMPANY
CERTIFIED PUBLIC ACCOUNTANTS

BROWNSVILLE, TEXAS
L. WM. LONG, C. P. A.
CARL S. CHILTON, JR, C. P. A.
IRVIN G. SHEPARD, C. P. A.
JIMMY L. STEELE, C. P. A.

HARLINGEN, TEXAS
FRANK S. HARDIN, C. P. A.

Board of Directors
International Supply Company, Inc.
Port Isabel, Texas

We have examined the Statement of Financial Position of International Supply Company, Inc. as of December 31, 19X1, the related Statement of Operations and Statement of Changes in Financial Position for the year then ended. Our examination was made in accordance with generally accepted auditing standards and accordingly included such tests of the accounting records and such other auditing procedures as we deemed necessary in the circumstances.

In our opinion, the accompanying financial statements present fairly the financial position of International Supply Company, Inc. as of December 31, 19X1 and the results of operations for the year then ended, in conformity with generally accepted principles of accounting applied on a basis consistent with that of the preceding year.

AUDITORS' COMMENTS

Review of operating results for the year - Your operating results for 19X1, compared with 19X0, are summarized below:

	19X1	19X0	Percent Increase (Decrease)
Sales	$ 645,609	$ 608,449	6.1%
Sales - shop	27,475	26,551	3.5%
TOTAL REGULAR SALES	$ 673,084	$ 635,000	6.0%
Special sale - merchandise		40,014	
	$ 673,084	$ 675,014	(.3%)
Gross profit - merchandise	$ 281,934	$ 244,759	15.2%
Gross profit - shop	7,076	7,126	(.7%)
Gross profit - special sales		2,001	
GROSS PROFIT COMBINED	$ 289,010	$ 253,886	13.8%
Operating expenses	247,872	226,635	9.4%
OPERATING PROFIT	$ 41,138	$ 27,251	51.0%
Miscellaneous income	3,797	4,388	(13.5%)
PROFIT BEFORE INCOME TAX	$ 44,935	$ 31,639	42.0%
Federal income tax	14,819	10,691	38.6%
NET PROFIT FOR THE YEAR	$ 30,116	$ 20,948	43.8%

Exhibit 4-4–Audit Report with Financial Review and Comments

PERCENT OF SALES

Gross profit - merchandise sales	43.67%	40.23%
Gross profit - special sales		5.00%
Operating expenses	36.83%	35.69%
Operating profit	6.11%	3.98%

These figures indicate an increase of 6.0% in sales (disregarding $40,014 in special sales in 1970) and 43.8% in net profit. The increase in net profit can be attributed primarily to two factors: the increase in sales volume, amounting to 6%, and an improvement in gross profit on merchandise sold. This latter reflected a marked increase, with gross profit jumping from 40.23% in 1970 to 43.67% of sales in 19X1. Gross profit increased 15% whereas sales volume increased 6%. Operating expenses increased $21,237, which is primarily attributed to salaries, bonuses and contribution to the profit sharing retirement fund. Expenses were up 9.4% from 19X1.

Review of changes in financial position during year - The financial statement of the company at December 31, 19X1, compared with one year earlier, is reflected below:

	December 31, 19X1	December 31, 19X0	Increase (Decrease)
Current assets	$ 342,360	$ 312,871	$ 29,489
Property and equipment (after depreciation)	22,428	24,364	(1,936)
Cash value of life insurance	20,220	18,909	1,311
	$ 385,008	$ 356,144	$ 28,864
Current liabilities	$ 86,944	$ 88,241	$(1,297)
Stockholders' equity	298,064	267,903	30,161
	$ 385,008	$ 356,144	$ 28,864
Working Capital	$ 255,416	$ 224,630	$ 30,786

The factors causing the increase in working capital are explained in the Statement of Changes in Financial Position on page 7.

Comparision of your company with industry averages for stores with sales of $500,000 to $750,000 is reflected below:

	INTERNATIONAL SUPPLY COMPANY 19X1	19X0	Industry Averages 19X0
Gross profit - merchandise	43.67 %	40.23 %	31.85 %
Gross profit - shop labor	29.53 %	30.93 %	32.02 %
Operating expenses	36.83 %	35.69 %	29.36 %
Net profit before income tax	6.96 %	4.88 %	4.03 %
Inventory turnover	1.93 times	2.33 times	2.79 times

Exhibit 4-4–Audit Report with Financial Review and Comments (continued)

Sales volume per employee (exclusive of shop)	$ 33,979	$ 38,145	$ 40,856
Current assets to current liabilities	3.94 to 1	3.55 to 1	2.32 59 1
Net profit on net worth	11.3 %	8.5 %	10.8 %

The following comments can be made concerning these comparisons:

1. Gross profit for 19X1 is 11.8% above average, whereas in the past several years it has been 10% above average. At the same time your inventory turn-over is below average. It is likely that you are buying in larger quantities and at better prices than average, thus causing both of the above conditions. Your inventory turnover declined as did the industry average; however, your decline was less than the industry average.

2. Gross profit on machine shop labor declined 1.40% while the industry average showed an increase of 6.50%.

3. Operating expenses have been higher than average for several years. During the current year you show a slight increase percentagewise. The industry average also increased slightly.

4. Your sales volume decreased by $4,200 per employee while the industry average showed an increase of $3,700.

5. Your ratio of current assets to current liabilities increased. This is reflected by the increase in working capital over the previous year. The increase in the current ratio is attributed to a $29,000 increase in cash and marketable securities. Current liabilities decreased by $1,000.

6. Net profit as a percentage of net worth has consistently run higher than industry averages and continues to do so. Your figure increased from 8.5% in 19X0 to 11.3% in 19X1 while the industry average increased from 4.8% in 19X9 to 10.8% in 19X0 - a substantial improvement.

LONG, CHILTON & COMPANY
Certified Public Accountants

Exhibit 4-4—Audit Report with Financial Review and Comments (continued)

MEMBERS AMERICAN INSTITUTE OF CERTIFIED PUBLIC ACCOUNTANTS

LONG, CHILTON & COMPANY
CERTIFIED PUBLIC ACCOUNTANTS

BROWNSVILLE, TEXAS
L. WM. LONG, C. P. A.
CARL S. CHILTON, JR, C. P. A.
IRVIN G. SHEPARD, C. P. A.
JIMMY L. STEELE, C. P. A.

HARLINGEN, TEXAS
FRANK S. HARDIN, C. P. A.

Board of Directors
Triangle Processing Company
Harlingen, Texas

The accompanying financial statements of Triangle Processing Company, Inc. have
been prepared from your accounting records. We have conducted a limited review
of your records, but have not performed an independent audit and therefore cannot express an opinion on the financial statements. Our comments and explanation
regarding your financial position and operating results are outlined as follows:

Review of operations for the year - The operating results for the year, compared
with the two prior years, are summarized below:

	19X9	19X8	19X7
Sales - processed product	$3,312,773	$3,123,910	$3,256,385
- outside product	1,546,868	1,341,800	2,073,813
- miscellaneous	108,453	123,774	108,986
	$4,967,912	$4,589,484	$5,439,184
Total expenses	$ 276,014	$ 288,092	$ 263,558
Net profit for the year	$ 61,211	$ 38,926	$ 39,066
Profit before depreciation	$ 88,226	$ 61,900	$ 64,447

Sales volume increased 8% in the current year while at the same time expenses were
decreasing 4%. This led to a substantial increase in net profit, amounting to 57%
over the prior year. The increase in profit, which was $22,285, is closely related
to reduction in two key expense categories, set forth below:

	THIS YEAR	LAST YEAR	DECREASE
Bad debts	$ 7,504	$ 25,331	$ 17,827
Interest expense	31,188	35,107	3,919

Several expense categories showed significant increases over the prior year, as
follows:

	THIS YEAR	LAST YEAR	INCREASE
Plant wages (overhead labor)	$ 54,974	$ 44,259	$ 10,715
Plant repairs	16,979	9,188	7,791
Depreciation	27,015	22,974	4,041

Exhibit 4-5—Unaudited Financial Statement Report
with Financial Review and Comment

Review of changes in financial position during the year - The financial position of the company at April 30, 19X9, compared with one year ago, is summarized below:

| | APRIL 30, | | INCREASE |
	19X9	19X8	(DECREASE)
Current assets	$ 457,913	$ 484,415	$(26,502)
Plant and equipment (after depreciation)	146,036	155,142	(9,106)
Other assets	965	965	-0-
	$ 604,914	$ 640,522	$(35,608)
Current liabilities	$ 239,370	$ 286,268	$(46,898)
Long term liabilities	116,882	128,062	'(11,180)
Deferred income	10,657	12,198	(1,541)
Stockholders' equity	238,005	213,994	24,011
	$ 604,914	$ 640,522	$(35,608)
Working Capital	$ 218,543	$ 198,147	$ 20,396

The factors causing the increase in working capital are summarized below:

Sources of working capital
> Profit before depreciation $ 88,226

Working capital was used as follows

Additions to buildings and equipment	$ 17,109	
Less long term financing	(5,612)	
	$ 11,497	
Reduction in long term debt	16,790	
Provision for dividends	38,000	
Reduction in deferred income	1,543	67,830
INCREASE IN WORKING CAPITAL		$ 20,396

Inventories are substantially lower than a year ago, causing a reduction in both current assets and current liabilities. Accounts receivable, however, were somewhat higher than a year ago. The increase in working capital has enabled the company to attain a current ratio of 1.9, compared with 1.7 last year.

A dividend of $38,000 was declared in January, 19X9. Of this amount, $13,500 was unpaid at April 30, 19X9 and this amount is reflected as a dividend payable.

Income tax status - The company has elected to be taxed under Subchapter "S" of the Internal Revenue Code, which provides that profits are reported for tax purposes by the stockholders.

> LONG, CHILTON & COMPANY
> Certified Public Accountants

**Exhibit 4-5—Unaudited Financial Statement Report
with Financial Review and Comment (continued)**

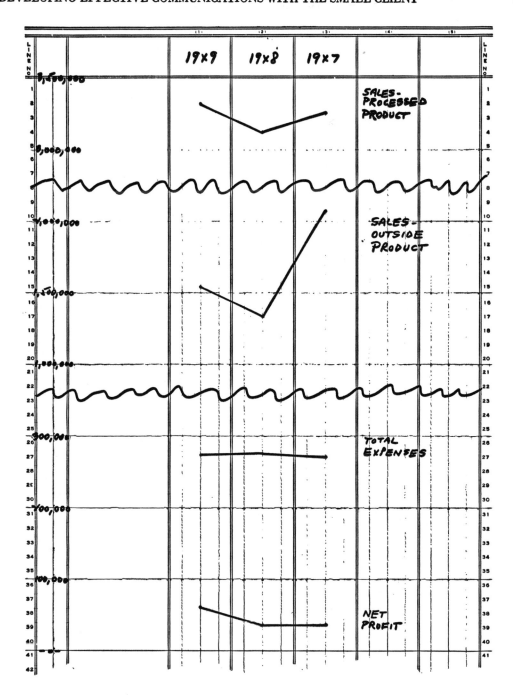

Exhibit 4-6–Trends in Sales, Expenses and Net Profit

CHAPTER 5

Developing and Managing a Top-Notch Practice

There are many facets to the makeup of a successful accountant and an ability to develop and manage the practice is among the more important. This chapter discusses various techniques that have been successfully used in this important area.

Practice Development

"Practice development" refers to efforts to increase the volume of the firm. An accounting firm needs to grow, because only through growth can opportunities be afforded to qualified people. A growing firm is able to employ and promote good people, which in return provides opportunities to serve larger clients, perform more challenging work and increase profits. Further, any accountant can expect to lose clients through mergers, death and other reasons, thus requiring new clients and new sources of revenue to make up these losses.

It is well established that one's own clients provide the best field for growth. Some practitioners tend to get so interested in obtaining new clients that they overlook present clients. Established clients can benefit from additional services and, indeed, should have the first priority. When thinking of practice development, remember that you owe your clients the best possible service and that they will be your best source of referrals.

Accountants who do best at practice development generally have a plan of action—a program for practice development. They know this provides better results than a hit-or-miss program.

The firm of Cheatham, Brady and Lafferty, which has offices in several Texas cities, has studied this matter carefully. Exhibit 5-1 is a memorandum issued by this firm to their partners and staff. The memo outlines the firm's philosophy regarding practice development, reasons for such a program, sources of new clients and a plan of action. Regular meetings are scheduled to review progress, discuss reasons for obtaining new clients or losing clients, and methods of broadening the firm's reputation in the community.

This plan is rather ambitious for the small firm or practitioner. The basic elements of practice development are clearly set forth, however, and can be adapted to a more modest plan. In our firm, for example, we review a list of clients gained and lost annually. The important point to remember is that anyone, regardless of size, will do better with a plan than without one.

Practice Management

Some accountants with growing practices do not devote sufficient time to management of the organization. Their normal objective is to perform client work and they find it difficult to devote non-chargeable time to management responsibilities. This is a tough hurdle to overcome but it has to be done. The writer knows this from experience.

Some firms try to solve the management problem by passing it around each year to a different partner. This is a sure way to poor management. The partner who inherits the job for the year will look upon it as an extra responsibility to be gotten out of the way as quickly as possible. Further, changes in management each year produce inconsistent procedures and methods of dealing with the staff. It is very difficult to have a smooth, continuing management function under this arrangement.

A sole practitioner naturally takes management responsibility in his firm, and partnerships should designate one partner as managing partner. The management function should be looked upon as a specialty, equally as important as technical specialties. The managing partner should study his specialty and work with it through the years.

There is a tendency to feel that the senior partner in the firm should always be the managing partner. The senior partner is a logical person based on experience, but it should be recognized that some people are not oriented toward management problems. Some partners are better suited for, and happier with, client work. The choice of a managing partner should, therefore, be based on the individual's aptitude and interest in management problems. If a younger partner can do the job, so be it.

Creating a Professional Image

The development of your practice is based to a considerable extent on what people think of you; on the image you present. Here are some guide lines to follow in creating your own professional image.

1. Reflect a desire to serve other people, showing a genuine interest in the problems of your clients and of your community.
2. Your standard of living should be in keeping with the image of a successful professional man.
3. Be self-confident, have a high opinion of yourself and of the value of your work.
4. Your office should be modern, comfortable and efficient.
5. Be known as a person who works on the professional level. Don't give the impression of doing detail work all the time.
6. Be known as a person on top of your job. Don't give the impression of continually being behind or snowed under.

People Make Your Practice Go

An accounting practice is as successful as the people who staff it. A group of talented people, properly managed and properly motivated, can make all the difference in the caliber of your service and the profitability of your practice. A most important management function relates to personnel; employing, training and motivating people.

It is well established that there is more to motivating people than an adequate salary. Money is important, of course, but other factors are equally so. People want to feel that their work is useful and important and to receive recognition for their efforts. They want to be treated as human beings and not as cogs in the wheel.

How do you accomplish this? Here are a few suggestions:

1. When an employee comes in to talk to you, stop what you are doing, look him in the eye, listen attentively and show an interest in what he is saying.
2. Give employees an opportunity to make suggestions, to be creative, and to make their ideas and personalities felt in the organization.
3. Provide adequate office facilities, including good lighting, good equipment, sufficient space, and private or semi-private offices wherever suitable.
4. Let the employee know how he is doing. At least once a year evaluate performance and discuss it. If possible, provide goals to reach during the next year. Don't forget compliments for jobs well done. On those occasions when it is necessary to be critical, do so with dignity and constructively.

Develop a system for obtaining information about the performance of partners and employees. One important measure of performance is fee production. The billings of the firm should be allocated among the various personnel performing the work. An analysis of fee production should be part of the monthly financial statement (see example in Exhibit 5-2).

Our firm uses two reports to evaluate the performance of partners. The first (Exhibit 5-3) reflects client responsibility carried by each partner as indicated by billings. We feel that one of a partner's primary duties is carrying a satisfactory load of client responsibility.

The second report evaluates each partner's ability to obtain a satisfactory fee on his billings. This report (Exhibit 5-4) accumulates write-ups and write-downs by partner through the year.

Learn All You Can from Others

It has been our experience that much of what we know about developing and managing our practice has come from other practitioners. The benefits of exchanging ideas with others cannot be obtained in any other way. Other practitioners are invariably willing to exchange ideas and discuss management policies and techniques. These matters can be discussed without revealing confidential information.

All practitioners should take advantage of attendance at professional meetings and seminars, and consider themselves fortunate to be members of a profession which provides opportunities to learn from others.

Evaluate Your Own Performance

What guidelines can you use to measure your own performance? In a sense, this can be done by reviewing the results of your efforts; increases in billings and profits of the firm. To probe deeper, however, you need to look at your performance in various areas of responsibility; fee production, public relations, clients' relations, technical expertise, management responsibility, relations with staff, etc.

The partners in our firm devised a list of various areas of partner responsibility on which we wanted to evaluate ourselves (Exhibit 5-5). This is recommended to any practitioner who wants to review his own performance in these important areas. An objective evaluation on an annual basis will help the accountant avoid complacency and keep him on his toes.

PRACTICE DEVELOPMENT

I. Reasons for a client development program

   A. Our office desires to grow in size in order to:
     1. Service larger clients
     2. Render broader client services
     3. Maintain high quality of service
     4. To increase firm's profitability

   B. We must acquire new clients in order to grow and to replace losses due to mergers, etc.

   C. To provide the income, fee volume, etc. for staff advancement.

II. Limitations on program

   A. We must at all times maintain and abide by the rules of professional conduct and the public accountancy laws of the various states. However, we can develop a very active and successful program within these professional concepts.

III. Sources of Growth

   A. Growth of present clients

   Though this category may seem at first to be out of our control it really isn't. Our program should include provisions for active participation in the areas of client growth by merger and expansion of geographic coverage.

   B. Additional services to present clients

   We must continue to strengthen our program of departmentalization and industry specialization to be able to develop the in-depth experts needed to diversify our services. However, we should continually review the needs of our clients to avoid overlooking an area of need which we can supply. Some specific areas to watch for and methods to use are:

     1. Pension and profit sharing plans, including Keogh Plans
     2. Estate planning
     3. Special audits not leading to an opinion, such as cash, inventory, and receivable audits.
     4. Systems design and changes
     5. EDP applications
     6. Budgeting
     7. Management letters with each audit
     8. Use of specialists
     9. Management audit questionnaire
     10. Assistance in financing

Exhit 5-1—Practice Development Program

C. Clients recommendations

This seems to be the source of a majority of new clients, therefore, it means that we must concentrate a large part of our efforts toward not just contented but enthusiastic clients. This can best be accomplished by having a genuine interest in the client and an understanding of his problems and needs. This can be compared to the "bedside manner" of a doctor and applies to all clients, large and small, because you never know where the next recommendation will come from.

We must plan our schedules to allow time to spend building a close personal relationship with as many of the present clients as possible. This can be done by:

1. Lunches
2. Visits by clients to our office
3. A friendly telephone call or visit
4. Parties at home
5. Outside entertainment, such as sporting events, hunting and fishing, theaters, etc.
6. Remembrances at birthdays, anniversaries, etc.
7. Client newsletter
8. Congratulatory letters
9. Directory of offices and affiliates
10. Holding of seminars and dissemination of business education material.

D. Recommendations from others

In order to develop business through friends and associates we must develop as wide an acquaintanceship as time and energy permit. This can be accomplished by participation in various organizations such as:

Religious and charitable
Civic
Social
Professional

It is not enough just to be a name in a roster. we must participate actively and hold positions of responsibility. We should begin immediately to develop and maintain a record of the various organizations and associations in which we have members and then to select others that we feel should be advantageous from the standpoint of client development and have partners or staff join them.

Some suggested organizations where we should particularly be known are:

Professional

1. National Association of Accountants
2. CPA Societies
3. Administrative Management Society

Exhibit 5-1—Practice Development Program (continued)

      4. American Management Association
      5. Systems and Procedures Association
      6. Business and Estate Planning Council
      7. Estate and Financial Forum
      8. Data Processing Managers Association
      9. Internal Auditors Association

Civic

      1. Chamber of Commerce
      2. Junior Chamber of Commerce
      3. Rotary, Kiwanis, Lions, etc.
      4. Political parties
      5. Neighborhood Civic Clubs

In addition to participation in the more or less formal organizations and associations, there are certain categories of business and professional people who are the best sources of referrals. Special efforts should be made to catalog present acquaintances and assiduously cultivate new ones in these groups. The most outstanding of these groups are:

      1. Attorneys
      2. Bankers
      3. Chartered Life Underwriters
      4. Security dealers
      5. Business executives
      6. Chief accountants and controllers, particularly CPA's in industry

IV. Operating procedures:

Meetings should be held as frequently as necessary to accomplish the objectives of the program but probably not less frequently than semi-monthly. In the beginning, the program should be developed among the partners but should ultimately be available to managers and others interested staff. The forms to be used are:

A. New Client Summary -
   This will be a continuing list of new clients prepared from the advice of contract forms, with the following column headings:

     Date
     Control Partner
     Client Number
     Client Name
     Type of business
     Type of engagement
     Source of engagement
     Estimated annual fee

B. Lost Client Summary -

   This will be a continuing list of clients lost, with the following column headings:

Exhibit 5-1—Practice Development Program (continued)

Date
Control Partner
Client Name
Approximate annual fee
Prospects for return
Reason for loss of account
Follow-up procedure

C. Practice Development Report –

This is a report of contacts made with people who are a potential
source of business, including present clients. It is to be maintained
by each partner and will have the following column headings.

Date
Person contacted
Title-function
Company/organization
Comments

D. A suggested agenda for these meetings is as follows:

1. Review new client summary
2. Review lost client summary
3. Review practice development report
4. Review and list prospective new clients
5. Review business section of newspapers
6. Review progress of cataloging acquantances among business
    and professional groups

E. Review progress of cataloging representation among business, civic
    and professional organizations.

Exhibit 5-1–Practice Development Program (continued)

LOST CLIENT SUMMARY

Date	Control Partner	Client	Approximate Annual Fee	Prospect For Return	Reason for Loss of Account	Follow-up Contact

Exhibit 5-1—Practice Development Program (continued)

NEW CLIENT SUMMARY

Control Partner	Client Number	Client	Type of Business	Engagement	Source of Engagement	Estimated Annual Fee

Exhibit 5-1—Practice Development Program (continued)

PRACTICE DEVELOPMENT REPORT

Name: _____   Period Ended _____

Date	Person Contacted	Title/Function	Company/Organization	Comments

Exhibit 5-1–Practice Development Program (continued)

LINE NO			CHARGEABLE HOURS (1)	(2)		BILLINGS (3)	(4)	(5)	LINE NO
			Current Month	Year to Date This Year	Last Year	Current Month	Year to Date This Year	Last Year	
1	Jones		156	600	549	1709	11764	8795	1
2	Brown		148	555	484	4834	17607	14317	2
3	Smith		160	534	547	4641	10779	9915	3
4	Bass		170	548	570	3873	10175	7085	4
5	Lyman		165	644	607	3938	14188	17134	5
6	Reed		717	836	737	7397	13061	10740	6
7	Wilson		708	845	831	1115	9935	8968	7
8	Black		701	854	833	869	9705	9706	8
9	Duncan		717	840	808	1895	7837	9873	9
10			1652	6756	5916	25766	103941	90528	10
11									11
12									12
13									13
14									14
15									15
16									16
17									17
18									18
19									19
20									20
21									21
22									22
23									23
24									24
25									25
26									26
27									27
28									28
29									29
30									30
31									31
32									32
33									33
34									34

Exhibit 5-2—Analysis of Fees Produced by Individuals

		Total	Jones	Brown	Smith	Lyman	
January		27906	5610	10666	2935	8615	1
February		25592	6526	4060	4495	10557	2
		53498	12136	14726	7390	19246	3
March		31732	12725	5673	6224	7110	4
		85230	24861	20399	13614	26356	5
April		42357	11841	17752	7096	10662	6
		127581	36702	33151	20710	37018	7
May		29181	7551	8648	7215	5767	8
		156762	44253	41799	27925	42785	9

Exhibit 5-3—Partner Responsibility as Reflected
by Client Billings

LINE NO			% of Total Billings	Jones	Brown	Smith	Lyman	LINE NO
1		January	5.7 %	312	86	352	⟨65⟩	1
2		February	.6	⟨769⟩	1707	⟨463⟩	⟨333⟩	2
3			3.0	⟨457⟩	2460	⟨111⟩	⟨398⟩	3
4		March	1.6	⟨742⟩	⟨588⟩	404	935	4
5			7.7	⟨699⟩	1972	793	537	5
6		April	4.8	443	1920	⟨763⟩	⟨73⟩	6
7			3.2	⟨756⟩	3892	30	464	7
8		May	7.1	⟨432⟩	313	⟨85⟩	740	8
9			3.0	⟨688⟩	4205	⟨55⟩	1704	9
10								10
11								11
12								12
13								13
14								14
15								15
16								16
17								17
18								18
19								19
20								20
21								21
22								22
23								23
24								24
25								25
26								26
27								27
28								28
29								29
30								30
31								31
32								32
33								33
34								34
35								35
36								36
37								37

Exhibit 5-4–Analysis of Net (Write-Downs) and
Write-Ups by Partner

Workload, Production and Firm Responsibility

1. Fees produced by partner's clients.
2. Profitability of work done for clients (writedowns, etc.).
3. Fees produced by partner individually.
4. Effectiveness in collecting client receivables.
5. Performance and up to date knowledge in basic areas of practice (tax, audit).
6. Performance and up to date knowledge in specialized areas (data processing, estate work, pension plan work, etc.).
7. Performance in contributing to the management of the firm.

Client Relations

8. Reputation for "attentive" service.
9. Ability of complete work promptly.
10. Availability to clients when needed.

Standing in the Community and the Profession

11. Image in the community as a top level citizen and professional man.
12. Positions of leadership in community organizations.
13. New clients brought in through individual contacts and efforts.
14. Standing within the profession (positions of leadership, etc.).

Exhibit 5-5—List of Partner Responsibilities

CHAPTER 6

Keeping Books
for the Small Client

There is no better way to get a "handle" on serving small clients than to offer to keep books for them. This is the service that small clients most frequently need, and it opens the door to a new market. Many firms, both large and small, are providing this service today. They do it because small business needs it and because it can be a profitable part of the practice. It also gets the accountant into circulation, thus helping to obtain new clients.

Accounting Requirements of Small Business

The owner of the average small business does not know how to keep books or prepare financial statements. Frequently, he will ask his wife to do the bookkeeping, or he may employ a bookkeeper who is not qualified. In any event, at the end of the year the accountant may be presented with an inadequate or poorly kept set of books and asked to prepare a tax return. He may spend as much time straightening out the books as would have been required to keep them himself.

In addition to the problem of not being able to get adequate bookkeeping personnel, the small business man has difficulty keeping up with the multitude of tax returns that must be filed. Payroll taxes, sales taxes and other reports must be prepared quarterly, and often require monthly deposits. It takes a capable bookkeeper to handle all these reports properly.

Faced with all his bookkeeping problems, the small businessman frequently asks his accountant to take over the whole job. By doing so, the accountant can do these things:

1. See that the books are properly kept.

2. See that all tax returns are properly prepared and timely filed.

3. See that current financial information is made available.

4. Provide financial advice and offer other services the client could use to advantage.

Upgrading Services to Bookkeeping Clients

When a professional accountant offers bookkeeping service, he should consider this work as a starting point for a higher level of service. The bookkeeping work should be a means to an end, and not the end itself.

It is difficult to get a proper fee from bookkeeping clients because of competition from bookkeepers who work at lower rates. Remember, however, that bookkeepers cannot offer all the skills and services of an accountant. Don't try to compete with the lower fees, but make your service worth your higher fee. And don't forget; try to help the client grow so that he will become an accounting or audit client.

Cast Yourself in the Right Role

Look upon yourself as serving a controllership function to the bookkeeping client. You are not only relieving the client of the chore of keeping books, you are also in a position to observe closely the financial health of his business. The client is busy with the daily problems of buying and selling, dealing with customers, dealing with employees and similar management problems. He probably lacks the training and experience to analyze financial statements for ratios and trends. Furthermore, he is not apt to have knowledge of internal controls, methods of financing, budgeting, and the like. Your experience in all of these areas puts you in a position to provide service with a value far beyond that of keeping books.

Play Your Role to the Hilt—It should be realized that many small business-men have no one with whom they can discuss their business problems. Taking cognizance of this you can make yourself even more useful if:

You are in frequent contact with your clients.

You are familiar with your clients' business operations.

You make yourself available to your clients to discuss business problems, whether they have to do with accounting and finances or not. Indeed, you should urge your clients to discuss their problems with you.

It is worth noting that the services being discussed here are management services. Professional literature has abounded in recent years with articles concerning the growing importance of management services in the practice of accounting. Here is an opportunity for the practitioner to get the feel of management services work and to develop skills in dealing with management problems as opposed to strictly accounting problems.

Specific Ways of Upgrading Services

Providing a higher level of service requires the practitioner to be in regular contact with the client. You can't do much for a client whom you see only once or twice a year.

The best way to see a client regularly is to provide him with a monthly financial statement, and review it with him each month. If it is not feasible to do this monthly, then it should be done at least quarterly. In some types of business, a full financial statement may not be needed as much as regular reports of major items of income or expense. In any event, every client needs certain financial information on a regular basis. A client who is not interested in financial reports at all will probably not be too successful, and it is questionable whether he should be accepted as a client.

In reviewing financial statements, the practitioner should be on the alert for any unusual trends. If a particular expense is getting out of line, if gross profit percent is running too low, if too much is being invested in equipment, the client should be warned. You can spot these things more readily than the client and it is your responsibility to point them out. Alerting your client to trends will, generally, earn his appreciation and respect.

Opportunities to Watch for.—If you hold regular meetings, the client will likely begin to bring up business problems for discussion. These discussions will provide you with opportunities to suggest additional ways you may serve your client, so be on the alert for them. The range of these services is limited only by the imagination and resourcefulness of the parties involved. A few illustrations are listed below.

1. Financing—Many small clients are in need of adequate financing. You can point out the difference between debt financing and equity financing, and can assist in locating and negotiating with interested parties.
2. Budgets—In the right circumstances, you can suggest that a budget be set up. This is especially helpful if the client has department heads or other employees who can influence income or expenses. It can also be valuable if there are other partners or stockholders. If the client decides on the use of a budget, you, the accountant, will naturally have the job of preparing it and comparing budget figures with actual results.
3. Review of operations—In certain cases where the company's operating results are unsatisfactory, you might suggest a series of weekly visits to the business to observe the operation more closely. Some objective of such visits might be to run a gross profit check on certain merchandise (cost vs. selling price), to observe if personnel seem to be properly utilized.

4. Personnel selection—Employing and keeping capable personnel is an important management function in which you can assist your clients. In time, you will gain considerable experience in the techniques of employing other personnel, both from employing people for your own office and helping clients locate bookkeepers. Know where to go to find applicants, how to conduct an interview, how to check references, and the like. If you can help your clients find the right people for the right jobs, they will be all the more convinced of your professional value.

5. Office equipment—You can serve as a consultant when the client needs office equipment by providing advice as to the types of equipment available, and recommending the most suitable type.

Seizing upon such opportunities can convert bookkeeping work into a truly professional service. The bookkeeping is only incidental—the starting point. By providing the more valuable services, not only will you earn the gratitude and respect of your client, but also the satisfaction of rendering the best possible service.

Special Problems Posed by Bookkeeping Services

A professional accountant who is offering bookkeeping services finds that he has some unique problems. Among them are:

1. The mass of routine detail in bookkeeping work.
2. Keeping up to date.
3. Keeping up with growing clients.

Handling the Detail Work

To a large extent bookkeeping work is routine and time consuming. Practitioners have gotten "snowed under" with it. The accountant should recognize the routine nature of bookkeeping work and try to avoid doing it personally. This is not possible for the practitioner who has no staff. But if he has to handle the entire assignment personally, he should do so as a temporary measure. His goal should be to relieve himself of the routine work as soon as possible by employing a staff or having the client's personnel perform the routine work.

Keeping up to Date

This is more of a problem than you might think. It is quite possible to obtain several bookkeeping clients in the space of a few months. If each new client requires several hours per month, the accumulated effect on your monthly workload is substantial.

There are devices you can use to make yourself stay up to date. Probably the most effective is to promise regular financial statements, preferably monthly. This practice has a number of advantages which will be discussed later, but it also has the distinct advantage of forcing you to keep up to date. Once a client has become accustomed to receiving regular financial statements, he will expect them at a certain time, and will "sound off" if the statement isn't received on time.

If the client does not want or need regular financial statements, the material for posting the books should still be brought in at regular intervals. If there is a regular rhythm to the work, it can be scheduled and accomplished more efficiently. A bad situation can develop when an agreement is made to keep a client's books for a monthly fee, the fee is paid monthly, but the work is postponed until the entire year has to be posted at once. This creates a bad impression on the client and creates scheduling problems in the accountant's office.

Keeping up with Growing Clients

Your bookkeeping clients should be reviewed regularly to see if any of them should be using their own bookeeeper. It is possible for an accountant to become so dependent on bookeeping work that he resists (perhaps unconsciously) any suggestion that a client employ a bookkeeper. This is a serious mistake, because the practitioner looses an opportunity to upgrade his practice. In fact, one of the goals in offering bookkeeping services should be to obtain clients who will grow too big for this service and then assist them in setting up their own bookkeeping staff, thus providing an opportunity for higher caliber service.

Along the same line, some clients try to impose more and more detail work on the accountant—work that should be done in the client's office. When this happens, you should suggest proper ways for the client to handle this work.

Avoid keeping accounts receivable ledgers and the like for clients, unless you have an organization to handle this work or use time-saving equipment. If you try to do it personally by manual posting methods, you will be getting involved in an unprofitable task.

Other clients will ask you to pay their bills for them. This can be as time consuming as accounts receivable work and such an arrangement should be entered into cautiously. Writing checks does not require the efforts of a professional accountant, and generally it is best if the client handles this work himself.

ORGANIZING YOUR PRACTICE FOR BOOKKEEPING WORK

Organizing and Operating the Service Efficiently

The practitioner needs to develop ability to supervise the work of other people. He must learn when to assign work to others, what work to assign, and how to supervise this work while it is underway and to review it when it is completed.

Developing an organization and making it function properly is one of the keys to success in the practice of accounting.

Choosing the Personnel

Men or women? The question of whether to employ men or women to handle the bookkeeping work is not easy to answer. Some argue strenuously for an accounting staff of nothing but men, while others prefer to employ a number of women. If young men out of college are to be employed, they can spend part of their time for the first years of employment in keeping books. This provides experience in a variety of small businesses. An accountant will not be satisfied with this type of work indefinitely and the firm must strive to grow fast enough to move him up to higher work.

Those who advocate the employment of women feel that they make steadier, more settled employees than do men. Generally, they are not as concerned with obtaining the CPA certificate and being moved up to doing audit and tax work, but are satisfied to continue handling bookkeeping work over the years. Further, male employees have been known to leave and open their own offices—taking some clients with them. This is not as likely to happen with female employees.

Appointing a Supervisor—When the bookkeeping work has grown to a point where there are three or four bookkeepers employed, a supervisor should be appointed. This could be a staff accountant who has supervisory talents. He should be responsible for the department except for some phases of client contact. The practitioner should be involved in certain phases of reviewing financial statements and tax planning and preparation.

Salary vs. Quality— If you are working alone, the employment of an assistant is a major expense item. When you're ready to hire a second person, it is still a major expense, but not quite as big a hurdle as was the first person. The firm is able to absorb each successive employee more readily. In the early stages of practice, there is a tendency to try to minimize this expense by employing people who do not command the best salary. This could prove to be a mistake.

An accounting firm has nothing to sell but service, and it takes people to render good service. You should resolve from the beginning to employ only people of high caliber. You will develop a better organization, give better service and have less problems and worries.

Supervising the Bookkeeping Work of Others

Certain techniques should be developed to aid you in supervising bookkeeping work.

A few of these are suggested below:

1. For new clients, handle most of the work yourself for the first two or three months. In this way, you get the feel of the books and become familiar with the problems. After this initial period, you are in a better position to assign the work to someone else.
2. Review check stubs each month to note any unusual transactions. Your employee can enter account numbers to be charged on the stubs, and you can review them in a few minutes.
3. One of the best ways to review the work of others is to prepare financial statements from books they have kept. Unusual or incorrect entries are easy to spot when doing this. Also, in preparing the statements yourself, you will come across points that should be discussed with the client—points that might be overlooked otherwise.
4. If you do not prepare financial statements, but have an employee do it, go over the statements. This step is part of your supervision under such circumstances. In this review, the statements should be compared with those of the preceding month, or perhaps the preceding year. If the client uses a budget, they should be compared with the budget. Such a comparison makes it easier to spot items that are out of line. It should be emphasized that this review is quite important, and should be done carefully and deliberately.

How to Assign Bookkeeping Work—Assigning work among your employees requires consideration of these questions:

1. Should an employee handle a client's work completely, including posting books, preparing quarterly tax reports, and preparing financial statements?
2. Should you use one employee to do payroll tax and sales tax reports for all clients in your office?
3. If you have a bookkeeping machine, should one employee be assigned to machine operation?

It can be observed that if you choose the method in question 1, you will reject the methods in questions 2 and 3— and vice versa. You will either make your employees "all around bookkeepers" handling the accounts all the way through—or, create some "specialists" in areas such as payroll tax reports or machine posting.

If the various employees are on a similar level of competence, and are capable bookkeepers, the method outlined in question 1 might be the best and obvious choice. If there is an employee who is especially good at machine posting, it might be well to have this person specialize in this area. There seems to be little point in having payroll tax reports all prepared by one person, since they are quite simple and each employee can prepare his own.

Whenever work is handed from one person to another—for whatever reason—there is some lost motion. Certain points must be discussed, and certain questions must be asked. When one person handles the whole job, this type of lost motion is minimized.

Type of Work the Accountant Should Do—If possible, your work for bookkeeping clients should be limited to these areas:

1. Supervision and review of others;
2. Conferences with the client;
3. Tax work;
4. Special assignments described earlier in this chapter.

Operating the Bookkeeping Service Efficiently

It is most desirable that your bookkeeping clients have a degree of uniformity in their record keeping. One feature of this would be to use uniform binders for the ledgers and journals, insofar as possible. Another feature could be in having the clients adopt a certain style of checks, check stubs, daily reports and so forth.

An important matter for you to consider recommending is the adoption of a uniform chart of accounts by your clients. A chart of accounts has several advantages. It keeps the bookkeeper from opening new accounts unnecessarily, and using account numbers is much preferable to using names. Also, assigning a number series to categories of accounts makes it easy to recognize the category of the account from its number.

The chart of accounts in Exhibit 6-1 is included as a guide. By using this or similar charts for all bookkeeping clients, you will have uniformity that will be helpful.

There are many other techniques that will increase your efficiency in providing bookkeeping services. These will be discussed in detail for the following types of bookkeeping systems:

1. Manual Systems
2. Bookkeeping Machine Systems
3. Data Processing Systems

Manual Systems

Manual bookkeeping as discussed here refers to a system where the posting is done by hand. The most conventional approach to this, of course, is to have journals where checks, daily reports and other transactions are entered, followed up by posting to a general ledger.

Advantages and Disadvantages—There are certain advantages to manual methods, primarily, the ease with which people can be instructed in their use. The use of bookkeeping machines and data processing equipment requires considerably more training of personnel than does manual posting. In manual systems, it is also easier to break up the work into different levels. Someone in your office can post the journals, then you can post the general ledger, if necessary. Further, you can arrange for portions of the posting to be done in your client's office, with the balance to be done in your own office.

The biggest disadvantages of manual bookkeeping are that it is time consuming and subject to clerical errors. Various shortcuts have been devised in order to save time. These shortcuts should be considered, but always with the view that the quality of the work cannot be sacrificed. Some general areas where shortcuts can be considered are listed below:

1. Eliminate monthly general ledger posting. This system works best if there is only one journal for all transactions. Total of this journal can be accumulated by month and carried forward. If the journal provides a sufficient columnar breakdown, an operating statement could be prepared from the totals. It would be a bit awkward to prepare a balance sheet, however. If no general ledger is maintained, the appropriate balance sheet figures could be prepared annually on a worksheet. This system should be used only for clients who are quite small.

2. Post directly to general ledgers. In some instances, it is feasible to post directly from check stubs to a general ledger, thus eliminating the journals. This could be done with contractors whose checks are charged to job accounts that are constantly changing. A drawback is that it is difficult to find an error in a ledger posted in this manner because of so many entries.

3. Eliminate recopying. There are many possibilities here; for example, it isn't necessary to copy the names of payees in the check register, since it is possible to go back to the check stub for this information. Some practitioners eliminate the check register entirely, running adding machine tapes on the canceled checks and posting from the tapes. Other records, such as sales invoices, lend themselves to the use of adding machine tapes. A great deal of time can be saved by such procedures.

When providing bookkeeping services to clients who use manual posting methods, serious thought should be given to the matter of shortcuts. Adopting suitable time-saving procedures, which do not penalize the quality of the records, can be a tremendous help in meeting the deadlines and the pressures of other work that will be present.

Bookkeeping Machine Systems

When the volume of bookkeeping work grows to a point where it is a full time job for two people, consideration should be given to acquiring a bookkeeping machine.

Advantages of Using a Bookkeeping Machine

1. Time-saving. A bookkeeping machine saves time in several ways, such as automatic totaling, elimination of certain journals, making it easier to balance, etc.
2. More uniformity. The machine posting of client's work in your own office will be more uniform than manual posting. This makes for a more efficient office set up.
3. Reduces cost of supplies. In some systems where a machine is used, the cost of supplies is reduced considerably over manual supplies.
4. More legible records. The records kept by a machine are much neater and easier to read.

Bookkeeping machines are available in many styles, sizes, and prices. The practitioner should review the market carefully to determine what suits his own needs best.

Typical System—The Central Supermarket records cash receipts and cash disbursements by means of a daily report. The daily reports, check stubs, bank statement and canceled checks and list of accounts payable are submitted monthly to the accountant.

The accountant maintains a machine-posted ledger for the store. The only records necessary are the general ledger (3 column sheets designed for machine posting) and the general journal (written by hand).

The accountant will review the daily reports in his office, and enter account numbers in red pencil for aid in posting. After these steps, each day's report is posted directly to the general ledger sheets. There is no journal, no totaling, no problem in balancing, since the machine will indicate any posting that is out of balance.

Check stubs are also reviewed and marked with account numbers. They are then posted directly to the general ledger account. As with the daily reports, the journal is again by-passed. Check numbers are also entered in the ledger accounts for identification purposes. Names of payees are not entered. The time saved in this step far exceeds any time later spent looking up check stubs for a payee's name. A typical ledger sheet reflecting deposits and checks is shown in Exhibit 6-2.

General journal entries are written by hand and posted to the ledger by machine. For financial statement purposes, accounts payable are set up by general journal entry and reversed out later by another entry.

Payroll records are also posted on the machine. In posting payroll records, it is helpful to have a machine with two or more totals, since there are several columns being posted. Without a sufficient number of totals, some of these columns will have to be added on an adding machine. On the other hand, if this is the only instance where several totals are needed, the additional cost of the larger machine might not be justified.

The general ledger, general journal and payroll records can all be kept together in a ring binder. Indeed, this is the only book needed for the Central Supermarket. It is a neat, legible record which is easily stored and easily used. The general journal sheet used in this case is illustrated in Exhibit 6-3.

In most machine bookkeeping setups, the ledger sheets are kept in trays. Trays, however, are not recommended for the accountant's office because several different sets of books would have to be kept in the same tray. Thus it would be too easy to insert ledger sheets into the wrong ledger by mistake. Use of ring binders will prevent this by a complete physical separation of each set of ledger sheets.

In addition to general ledger and payroll records, certain other work can be performed on the machine. While it is generally recommended that accounts receivable work should not be undertaken, there are instances where it is desirable to do so. A machine operation is ideal for accounts receivable work.

There may be instances where the accountant prepares the client's payroll checks. A machine operation can be set up to prepare the checks and post the payroll records simultaneously.

Disadvantages of a Machine System

1. If there is considerable turnover of personnel, training people to operate the machine can become a chore. While most bookkeeping machines are fairly easy to operate, a certain amount of training is necessary, and practice for a period of some weeks is required before the operator becomes fast and proficient.
2. If the machine breaks down, no work can be done until it is fixed. The availability of prompt service should be investigated before a machine is purchased. If repairs are made promptly, the problem is minimized. It can be readily understood, however, that the practitioner cannot have a machine sitting idle for several days before someone fixes it. Generally, it is best to enter into a service contract with the manufacturer.
3. A machine system is not as flexible as a manual system in transferring work between employees. Ordinarily there will be several people in the office who do not use the machine (typists, secretaries, partners, etc.). When work falls behind schedule, some of these people will help to catch up. If they have not learned machine posting, or are out of practice, they cannot help.

The disadvantages of the machine system can be overcome easily by proper use of personnel, service contract arrangements for machine repairs, and the like. The advantages far exceed the disadvantages. With proper use of a machine system, a great volume of bookkeeping work can be handled promptly and neatly right in your own office.

Data Processing System

More and more professional accountants are taking advantage of modern developments by introducing some type of data processing equipment into their offices. When satisfactory plans for such a system have been made, the advantages are generally numerous and striking—and are particularly applicable to bookkeeping work. Some accounting firms that previously declined bookkeeping work have reversed their position and entered the field using data processing equipment.

The use of such equipment eliminates much of the detail in bookkeeping work, speeds up the issuance of financial statements, and provides the client with data that would not be feasible to collect otherwise.

The most popular arrangement has been for the practitioner to purchase an adding machine that produces a punched paper tape—a machine commonly called an "add-punch." The client's transactions are entered into the machine which produces the tape. The tape is then sent to a service bureau where it is processed, producing a written record of the transactions for the period, a trial balance, financial statements, and any other material that may be desired. A portion of a typical trial balance prepared on data processing equipment is shown in Exhibit 6-4. In this system, the trial balance serves as the general ledger.

Factors to Consider—Changing from a conventional setup to the add-punch type of operation is a step which must receive much deliberate consideration. It represents a major decision and a considerable departure from the traditional ways of doing things. Some of the factors that should be considered are discussed below.

1. Your present bookkeeping clients should be analyzed to determine which can be converted to a data processing system. While the majority probably could be converted, there are always those with special problems, complicated situations, and so on that will be handled more satisfactorily by some other method.
2. Client reaction should be determined. The use of a service center requires sending the material out of the accountant's office. While arrangements can be made to identify clients by number instead of name, this is a situation that will have to be explained carefully to clients. Also, some clients feel more secure if they know they have a set of books—something they can see and feel. In the minds of some, the worksheet type records obtained from the service bureau would not be quite the same as a set of books.

   Another problem is the appearance of financial statements prepared by data processing equipment. Their appearance does not compare favorably with those prepared on an electric typewriter and run off on an offset printing machine. The accountant must either educate clients to accept statements prepared by the service bureau, or must re-type them in his office—thereby losing some of the labor-saving advantage the equipment affords. A statement prepared by a service bureau is illustrated in Exhibit 6-5.

3. The selection of a service center is most important. The accountant must carefully consider the center's location, reliability, and prices. These points will be discussed later in this section.

4. An add-punch machine or other type of "input" equipment must be acquired. Review the various types and models available to determine which is the most suitable.

5. Personnel in your office should not be overlooked. Will they look upon this change as a device which will save them hours of tedious detail work and make their jobs more interesting? Or will they fear that automation is a threat to their jobs? Employees resistance can disrupt the program, and they must be convinced of the value of the change.

Preparing Material for Processing—One early decision you must make is whether the tape should be prepared in your office or in the client's office. Tied in with this is whether the preparation should be done by your personnel or the client's.

Where to Perform the Work—The most satisfactory procedure seems to be for the work to be done in your office by your personnel—for bookkeeping work, at least. The smaller bookkeeping clients generally cannot and need not purchase their own add-punch machines—their need does not justify this. Nor do they have employees who would do a good job of operating the equipment. You, by providing both the machine and the personnel, can utilize both to better advantage.

It also has been found generally that it is best to leave the machine in your office. Although the machine can be moved about, most models are somewhat larger and heavier than regular adding machines, thus discouraging too much moving about. It is generally best to bring the documents to the machine, rather than vice versa.

Source Data Needed—In performing a full bookkeeping service for a small client, the check stubs, canceled checks, deposit tickets, daily reports and other material are brought to the accountant's office. It is helpful if the client codes as many check stubs as possible with the account numbers of the chart of accounts—but this is not imperative. It is imperative, however, regardless of who does the work, that the coding be accurate so that the correct account numbers are punched into the tape.

Performing the Work—How the various transactions are entered on the add-punch machine (but with some variations, possibly between makes of machine) is described in the following paragraphs.

An entry is made by punching the figures on the adding machine for the appropriate references, depressing the non-add key. Then the amount is placed in the machine. A debit is a plus and a credit is a minus. As an illustration, if check number

1234 for $427.15 is being charged to account 1131, the adding machine tape would appear as follows:

$$123411.31 \text{ N (non-add)}$$
$$427.15 \quad \text{(plus)}$$

When all checks have been punched, a total is obtained and entered as a credit to the bank account.

Fixed information such as month, year and journal source number is entered one time only and automatically repeated throughout the run.

Split transactions, those having several account numbers and/or debits and credits, can be handled in much the same manner. It is only necessary to indicate separately the account number and the amount for each element of the transaction, with a plus or minus entry to designate the debit or credit.

Check the tape after it has been completed to see if all entries are correct for both account number and amount. Whenever an error is found, it is corrected simply by entering the appropriate ledger account number and reversing the dollar amount. The correct entry is then punched into the tape.

A reasonably proficient operator can enter 300 transactions an hour. Compare this with the manual entry of 300 transactions in journals, posting to a general ledger and preparing financial statements, and it is readily seen that the time saved by keeping books in this manner is substantial.

Other Applications—In addition to journals, trial balances, financial statements and payroll records can be produced. To do this, the practitioner merely runs a separate tabulation on the add-punch machine of the payroll data. The service bureau then proceeds to keep employees' earnings records, and to prepare payroll tax reports including W-2 forms at the end of the year.

Similarly, accounts receivable and accounts payable subsidiary ledgers and statements can be obtained as by-products of the entry of sales, cash receipts and disbursements, and purchases. This is accomplished by assigning account numbers to vendors and by entering these codes along with the regular material. If desired, the service bureau can prepare statements for customers.

Procedures also can be set up for doing a partial bookkeeping job. The various journals (cash receipts, for example) can be posted by the client and then turned over to the accountant, who will punch the totals and adjustments into the tape. This material is sent to the service center where the trial balance and financial statements are prepared.

Some accountants use a punched card system which is similar to that described in the preceding paragraph. The journals, usually posted by the client, are sent to the accountant who reviews the work and makes necessary adjusting entries. The service center punches cards to record the entries, and prepares a trial balance and financial statements. Practitioners who use this method find that it has advantages similar to that of the add-punch system and requires no investment in equipment. The system has its best application, however, where the client posts the journals.

Selection of a service bureau—Since most accountants do not find it feasible or desirable to purchase their own computer or tabulating equipment, a service bureau performs this work for them. The selection of a service bureau is a key to the success of the entire data processing venture. The practitioner must locate a service bureau which is dependable, accessible, and reasonable in cost. There must be a close and harmonious relationship between the accountant and his service bureau.

Must the service center be close at hand? Some accountants use service bureaus located hundreds of miles away from their offices and find this quite satisfactory. A few years ago, there were a limited number of bureaus and those who wanted to use one frequently had to send the material quite a distance. Also, certain larger service bureaus have more advanced equipment, provide excellent service, charge modest rates and, therefore, can attract customers from a wide area.

Each year, however, more and more local bureaus open for business. In most parts of the country you should be able to find one reasonably close at hand. Some prefer to work with a service bureau that is accessible in person or by telephone. They find that it is much easier to get errors corrected and to discuss problems. However, local bureaus often have limited equipment and know-how and may charge higher than average rates. Consequently, you should check on both local and area-wide bureaus.

Standards the service center should meet. Before entering into an arrangement, the service bureau should be asked for a trial run. This can be limited or fairly extensive depending on the circumstances. During a trial run, you can check several things.

1. Reliability. The reliability of the material received should be studied carefully. If errors show up, it must be determined whether they are your fault or the bureau's. If these problems cannot be resolved during a trial run, then another bureau should be considered.
2. Promptness. A trial run will give some idea of the length of time required to get material processed. This is quite important, since clients receiving monthly financial statements are not inclined to wait too long.
3. Cost. Each run, if it is being done gratis or at reduced rates, should contain the amount of the charge at regular rates. Service bureaus state charges at so much per transaction, but have different ways of figuring the number of transactions. Some charge for cards and supplies separately, others do not. All aspects of this should be checked.

Good service bureaus are available. The practitioner who wants to go to data processing must take the time to find a good one and develop a close working relationship with it.

Additional Applications for Add-punch Equipment—The practitioner who acquires add-punch equipment will find that he can do more with it than bookkeeping work. Some of the applications are outlined below.

The general ledger and financial statements of many larger clients can be processed with this equipment. Further, some clients want such extensive departmental expense figures that it is impractical to try to produce them with a manually posted general ledger. Arrangements can be made to produce a punched tape of the client's journals from which many expense breakdowns can be handled economically. The service bureau can prepare operating figures or expense reports in most any format desired.

For example, it is possible to analyze sales invoices in a number of ways—by product, by location, by salesman. You simply take the invoices and punch the appropriate data into the tape.

Perpetual inventory records can also be produced. Merely put quantity data on purchases and sales invoices into the add-punch machine, and the service bureau produces the inventory control reports.

Other uses of this equipment undoubtedly have been discovered. The add-punch machine is opening up an entire new area of service to you, both by eliminating the detail work of bookkeeping and by enabling you to provide management with information and reports that are not feasible otherwise.

Disadvantages of Data Processing Systems—The description of the advantages of data processing system may lead the reader to decide that this setup will solve all his problems. It is true that many practitioners are using this equipment enthusiastically. It is also true that some have investigated and decided to stay with conventional methods. Others have tried it and abandoned the idea. These disadvantages, therefore, should be outlined.

Difficulties with service bureaus—Service bureaus have been a problem that some accountants have not been able to overcome. In some cases, the service bureau could not turn out work promptly enough to meet the demands of the accountant and his clients. Processing costs have been too high for some accountants. Others have found it difficult to get errors corrected. When there is an undetected error in the tape, the financial statements will contain the error and must either be re-run (at additional cost) or corrected the next month.

When source data is not available—Year-end closings have presented difficulties. Some clients take two or three months to price their inventories, thus throwing the whole program behind. It is more difficult to handle this situation in a data processing system than it is in a conventional system. Either the source material must be held in abeyance for machine entry after the year-end closing or, if entered currently, the tapes must be held for later processing. Generally, it is best not to process until the opening balances are available.

Employee problems with the machine—The machine itself has caused problems. Some have found the add-punch to be so noisy that the whole office is disrupted. Others have discovered employee resentment to the automation process, thus jeopardizing the whole venture. In some instances, employees have blamed the machine for human errors, causing clients to demand that their accounts be taken off punched tape.

Client's problems with the machine—Some have found that too many of their clients were not suited to a punched tape application. When clients send in material that is inaccurate, it is often too risky to go the add-punch route. Other clients have such involved problems that their books can be handled better by conventional methods. Also, some clients are always behind, making it difficult to work out a regular schedule with the service bureau.

When questions arise about prior operations. Analyzing prior records is often difficult. Upon examination by the Internal Revenue Service and others, or upon request for certain information from the client, you generally have to spend more time in looking up material or explaining the system.

These disadvantages can be overcome, and have been overcome by numerous practitioners. When contemplating data processing, being aware of the bad as well as the good points will help in making your decision.

Acquiring Your Own Data Processing Equipment—The preceding sections of this chapter have assumed that the accountant would use a service bureau for processing. In most instances, this is the best approach. The service bureau, by serving a number of customers, can utilize the fairly expensive processessing equipment to best advantages.

There are accountants, however, who have set up a full data processing system—creating, in effect, their own service bureau. They found that they can better serve their clients by operating this equipment themselves.

There are two main types of processing equipment—conventional tabulating equipment and electronic computers. Both types can be found in accounting offices. The major factors to be considered in deciding to buy or lease one type or another are discussed in the following pages.

Tabulating Equipment—Tabulating equipment, sometimes called "punch card equipment," has been in use for many years. The equipment has no memory capability, but simply reads cards that are fed through it. In the 1940's and early 1950's, nearly all data processing was done with punch card equipment. The larger and more sophisticated users, however, have long since turned to computers. There is, therefore, a great deal of tabulating equipment available today at a very reasonable cost.

This equipment is well suited to the accountant with a volume of book-keeping work. The program is flexible and it is easy to make changes and corrections in trial balances and financial statements. The equipment will handle a great variety of general accounting applications, as well as payroll and accounts receivable work. Auxiliary equipment which will perform calculations can be added.

The greatest attractions of tabulating equipment are their flexibility and the cost. The cost factor is somewhat offset, however, by the fact that less "card handling" is required in some of the newest small computers. This later equipment, therefore, can be operated with a more limited personnel.

Computers—The variety of computers available today is enough to bewilder the accountant. The size, cost and capability vary tremendously. Most accountants will be interested in the smaller models. The newer small computers offer many attractive features at a price within the range of numerous practitioners. They will perform all the work done by bookkeeping machines and tabulating equipment, plus handling other jobs, and do it faster.

Since computers have been around for quite a few years, it is possible to lease or rent one of the older models. Here it is possible, as with tabulating equipment, to obtain at less cost an older machine, but one which will still do a first rate job.

Some firms have found that their computer operation has experienced rapid growth and has become one of the more important parts of their practice. It is entirely possible to get into extensive work in fields that were not originally anticipated.

Personnel—Data processing people are highly skilled and specialized. In many parts of the country, they are in short supply and command high salaries. A practitioner contemplating acquiring his own data processing equipment should first determine the availability and cost of personnel.

Start-up Costs—Most accountants who have entered such a program have encountered an initial period when losses were incurred. The practitioner who installs his own equipment should, therefore, be prepared to support the program financially in the initial phases.

TECHNIQUES AND POINTERS FOR MAXIMUM EFFECTIVENESS

Streamlining the Preparation of Financial Statements

The desirability of preparing regular financial statements for each bookkeeping client has been discussed previously. This provides a higher level of service and gives you an opportunity for frequent contact with the client.

Preparing financial statements, however, requires a considerable amount of time, and can run up the cost of providing service. In some cases, preparing the statement will require as much time as posting the books for a month.

The preparation of financial statements for a bookkeeping client involves the following additional work.

1. Adjusting entries are prepared and posted;
2. The statement is prepared from the books or from a worksheet;
3. The statement is typed;
4. The typed statement is checked;
5. The desired number of copies are run off on a machine;
6. The copies are assembled and bound;
7. The statement is mailed or delivered.

Four Time-Saving Techniques

While there is a considerable amount of time involved in preparing statements, there are also opportunities for saving time. Some of these are outlined below.

Adjusting-Entry Shortcuts—Some monthly adjustments can be reflected in the financial statements without being recorded in the books. If, for instance, depreciation will run about $6,000.00 per year, depreciation expense on the operating statement and the reserve for depreciation on the balance sheet can be increased $500.00 each month without recording the adjusting entries. Changes in inventories can be computed each month on the cost-of-sales worksheet—or the cost of sales can be computed on the statement itself. It is not necessary to record the monthly inventory changes on the books.

Many adjustments can be set up so that they remain the same each month, The amortization of prepaid insurance, for example, can be recorded as an estimated figure for the monthly statements, and adjusted to the end of the year.

Set Up Blank Statements—If your procedure is to prepare the statement each month by hand, considerable time can be saved by having the heading and account titles already set up on the pencil copy. If you have duplicating equipment, worksheets can be run off with everything filled in except the dates and figures. These should not be prepared beyond one year in advance, since there usually will be enough changes in account captions to require new forms. Also, space should be left for new account titles to be added. Such worksheets will save 30 minutes to an hour in the preparation of most financial statements.

In addition to saving time, the statement can be useful in reflecting trends. The statement is set up so that figures for the next succeeding month are added to the next column. Our firm prepares a statement for some clients similar to the one shown in Exhibit 6-6. In addition to reflecting trends in the client's operations, the statement is delivered to the client earlier in the month, since it is not typed. Note also that the pennies have been dropped. This speeds up the preparation and, more importantly, makes it easier for the client to read.

Other firms have gone more extensively into the use of trend type statements. Mr. Aaron M. Rose, CPA of Philadelphia, has developed the fine example found in Exhibit 6-7. The report is typed on a master and photocopied. The firm delivers the reports in a special cover, with instructions as to filing it in a ring binder.

The statement in Exhibit 6-7 presents a statistical comparison of both the previous years figures as well as with the budget. This imaginative reporting portrays the work of the accountant at its best. Certainly the management of this company should be well informed.

Put the Bookkeeping Machine to Work—Your bookkeeping machine can also be used to prepare statements. The headings are printed or typed in, and the figures can be inserted by the machine. The machine automatically does the necessary adding and subtracting. This system works best where the format of the statement is somewhat simple, and where a small number of copies is needed.

Use an Automatic Typewriter—Typewriters are available which can automatically type certain material. Such equipment is being used by some accounts for preparing financial statements.

The first time a financial statement is prepared, it is typed in the usual manner. The typewriter automatically punches a paper tape which "captures" the material being typed. The next time the statement is typed, the typewriter "reads" the punched tape and automatically types everything except the figures. The typewriter automatically stops at the places where dollar amounts are to be entered, and these are entered by the typist. Automatic typing is done at a speed of 100 words per minute.

Practitioners who have installed this equipment report that typists can produce two or three times as many financial statements as with a conventional typewriter. Also, the tape can be revised quite easily to take care of changes in the format that occur from time to time. This equipment can be used for regular monthly or quarterly financial statements, for payroll tax reports and other operations.

Another application is in preparing additonal copies of any report. When the first copy is prepared, the typist can produce a punched tape that contains both the format and the dollar amounts. To produce additional copies, simply run the tape through the machine again—no operator effort at all is involved.

Your Understanding with the Client

One final word—and an important one. Be sure your client knows you are doing bookkeeping work, not auditing work. There have been instances where accountants have been sued by a bookkeeping client because an embezzlement was not discovered. This may sound ridiculous, but it has happened.

The wise accountant will adopt a policy of requiring an engagement letter for each new bookkeeping client (see Exhibit 6-8). The letter should outline all pertinent points, such as fee arrangement, but most importantly should specify than the services being rendered are bookkeeping services, not auditing services, and cannot be relied upon to disclose embezzlements and shortages.

Also be sure that all financial statements are clearly marked "unaudited" and that all required disclosures are made. The profession requires that all financial statements bearing an accountant's name, even though unaudited, disclose such matter as contingent liabilities, long term leases, accounting policies and the like.

It has been the purpose of this chapter to show how you can profitably extend bookkeeping service, using this service as a stepping stone toward higher level accounting work. The techniques presented are those which have been effective in providing good service, and through this service showing clients how good records can help them in running their businesses.

Various methods and approaches have been discussed, each with special application. Study them yourself, and select those which will fit your situation best.

Client Name_____Act. NO._____

CHART OF ACCOUNTS

CURRENT ASSETS - 100

CASH 100-129
- 100 - Cash on hand
- 101 - Petty cash fund
- 102 - _____
- 103 - _____
- 104 - _____
- 105 - Cash on deposit - FNB
- 106 - Ch on dep-PASB
- 107 - Ch on dep-NBC
- 108 - Ch on dep-MMSB
- 109 - Ch on dep-LFSB
- 110 - Ch on dep-Payrl Acct.
- 111 - _____
- 112 - _____
- 113 - _____
- 114 - _____
- 115 - _____
- 116 - Ch on dep-BS&LA
- 117 - _____
- 118 - _____
- 119 - _____

RECEIVABLE - 130-149
- 130 - Acct receivable-trade
- 131 - Acct rec-NSF cks
- 132 - Acct rec-employees
- 133 - Crew advances
- 134 - Notes rec.
- 135 - Allw for doubtf acct
- 136 - _____
- 137 - _____
- 138 - _____
- 139 - _____

INVENTORIES - 150-169
- 150 - Merchandise invent
- 151 - Trading stamp invent
- 152 - Jobs in progress
- 153 - _____
- 154 - _____
- 155 - _____
- 156 - _____
- 157 - _____
- 158 - _____
- 159 - _____

PREPAID EXPENSES - 170-189
- 170 - Prepaid insurance
- 171 - Prepaid interest
- 172 - Prepaid franchise tax
- 173 - Prepaid serv. contract
- 174 - Ch value of life ins
- 175 - Ins. premium deposit
- 176 - Dep on plans

- 177 - _____
- 178 - _____
- 179 - _____
- 180 - _____
- 181 - _____

FIXED ASSETS - 200

- 200 - Buildings
- 201 - _____
- 202 - _____
- 203 - _____
- 204 - _____
- 205 - _____
- 206 - Equipment
- 207 - Furniture and fixtures
- 208 - Office equipment
- 209 - Plant equipment
- 210 - Autos & trucks
- 211 - Air con equipment
- 212 - Kitchen equipment
- 213 - Paving
- 214 - Paving, st., rdways
- 215 - Guest room furnishings
- 216 - Banquet rm furnishings
- 217 - Landscaping
- 218 - _____
- 219 - _____
- 220 - _____
- 221 - _____
- 222 - _____
- 223 - _____
- 224 - _____
- 225 - Boats
- 226 - _____
- 227 - Allw for depreciation
- 228 - _____
- 229 - _____
- 230 - _____
- 231 - _____
- 232 - Land
- 233 - _____

OTHER ASSETS - 300

- 300 - Organization expense
- 301 - Loan expense
- 302 - Goodwill
- 303 - Utility deposits
- 304 - _____
- 305 - _____
- 306 - _____
- 307 - _____
- 308 - _____

- 309 - _____
- 310 - _____
- 311 - _____
- 312 - _____
- 313 - _____

CURRENT LIABILITIES - 400

- 400 - Accts payable
- 401 - _____
- 402 - _____
- 403 - _____
- 404 - _____
- 405 - _____
- 406 - _____
- 407 - _____
- 408 - _____
- 409 - _____
- 410 - _____
- 411 - _____
- 412 - _____
- 413 - _____
- 414 - _____
- 415 - _____
- 416 - _____
- 417 - _____
- 418 - _____
- 419 - _____
- 420 - _____
- 421 - _____
- 422 - SS Tax Pay-employee
- 423 - SS Tax Pay-employer
- 424 - Withholding Tax Pay
- 425 - Withldg Tax Deposits
- 426 - T.E.C. Payable
- 427 - F.U.T. Payable
- 428 - _____
- 429 - _____
- 430 - State Sales Tax Pay
- 431 - St Occupancy Tx Pay
- 432 - Fed Excise Tx Pay
- 433 - _____
- 434 - Acrd Rent Payable
- 435 - Accr Property Tax
- 436 - Accr Interest
- 437 - Accr Salaries
- 438 - Accr Income Tax
- 439 - Accr Workmen's Comp.
- 440 - _____
- 441 - _____
- 442 - _____
- 443 - Note Pay-FNB (Only for short term notes - No installments notes)

Exhibit 6-1—Chart of Accounts

444 - Note pay PASB
445 - _____
446 - _____
... - _____
448 - _____
449 - _____
450 - _____

LONG TERM LIABILITIES - 500

500 - _____
501 - _____
502 - _____
503 - _____
504 - _____
505 - _____
506 - _____
507 - _____
508 - _____
509 - _____
510 - _____
530 - Unrealized profit -
      installment sales

CAPITAL - 600

601 - Capital account
602 - Personal withdrawals
603 - Deductible withdl
604 - Income Tax withdl
605 - _____
606 - _____
607 - _____
608 - _____
609 - _____
610 - _____
611 - _____
612 - _____
630 - Capital stock authzd
631 - Cap stk unissued
632 - Cap stk outstanding
633 - Cap surplus
634 - _____
635 - _____
636 - Retained earnings
637 - Undistributed taxable
      income
638 - _____
639 - _____

INCOME - 700

700 - Sales
701 - _____
702 - _____
703 - _____
704 - _____
705 - _____
706 - _____
707 - _____

708 - _____
709 - _____
740 - Sales Returns
741 - Sales Discounts
750 - Misc Income
751 - Bad debts recovered

COST OF SALES - 800

800 - Purchases
801 - _____
802 - _____
803 - _____
804 - _____
805 - _____
806 - _____
807 - _____
808 - _____
809 - _____

840 - Purchases Returns
841 - Purchases Discounts

850 - Freight

860 - Inventory Variance

EXPENSES - 900

900 - Salaries
901 - Salaries - officers
902 - _____
903 - _____
904 - _____
905 - _____
906 - _____
907 - _____
908 - Advertising
909 - _____
910 - Auto & truck
911 - _____
912 - Bad debts
913 - Bank service charge
914 - _____
915 - Ch over & short
916 - _____
917 - Depreciation
918 - _____
919 - Donations
920 - _____
921 - Dues and subscriptions
922 - Entertainment
923 - _____
924 - _____
925 - Insurance
926 - _____
927 - _____
928 - _____
929 - Interest
930 - Laundry

931 - Legal & accounting
932 - _____
933 - Misc
934 - Office supplies
935 - _____
936 - _____
937 - Postage
938 - _____
939 - Rent
940 - _____
941 - Repairs
942 - _____
943 - _____
944 - Store supplies
945 - Shop supplies
946 - _____
947 - Taxes & licenses
948 - Taxes - Payroll
949 - Taxes - other
950 - _____
951 - Telephone
952 - _____
953 - Travel
954 - Travel & entertainment
955 - _____
956 - Utilities
957 - _____
958 - _____
959 - _____
960 - Wages
961 - _____
962 - _____
963 - _____
964 - _____
965 - _____
966 - Captain share
967 - Crew share
968 - Crew groceries
969 - Ice
970 - Fuel
971 - Ice & fuel
972 - Nets
973 - New nets
974 - Net repairs
975 - Supplies
976 - Repairs
978 - Processing
979 - _____
980 - _____
981 - _____
982 - _____
983 - _____
984 - _____
985 - _____
986 - _____
988 - _____
989 - _____
990 - _____
991 - _____
992 - _____

Any account No. can be expanded for locations and departments by use of one or two additional
digits. SS must be 422-WH must be 424-Salaries and/or wages must be in the 900 series acct Nos.

Exhibit 6-1—Chart of Accounts (continued)

LEDGER

NAME

ADDRESS

REMARKS

Cash on deposit - Pan American State Bank

DATE	REFERENCE	CHARGES	M	CREDITS	V	BALANCE
BALANCE FORWARDED						815.27
JAN 11'65		1,407.00 +				
JAN 20'65		239.76 +				
JAN 25'65		1,760.43 +				
FEB 15'65		1,538.92 +				
MAR 11'65		497.75 +				
MAR 29'65		787.00 +				7,046.13 ●
JAN 4'65				20.00 -		
FEB 1'65				20.00 -		
MAR 1'65				20.00 -		6,986.13 ●
JAN 2'65	1,217			50.00 -		
JAN 2'65	18			50.00 -		
JAN 2'65	19			24.42 -		
JAN 5'65	1,220			64.54 -		
J 2'65	21			92.83 -		
JAN 12'65	22					
JAN 12'65	23			50.00 -		
JAN 13'65	24			100.00 -		
JAN 14'65	25			381.23 -		
JAN 14'65	26			281.00 -		
JAN 14'65	27			150.00 -		
JAN 15'65	28			90.80 -		
JAN 15'65	29			161.88 -		
JAN 15'65	1,230			346.05 -		
JAN 23'65	31			21.00 -		
JAN 23'65	32			349.83 -		
JAN 23'65	33			20.00 -		
JAN 23'65	34			248.88 -		
JAN 23'65	35			479.05 -		
JAN 27'65	36			100.26 -		
JAN 27'65	37			18.71 -		
JAN 27'65	38			44.56 -		
JAN 27'65	39			8.91 -		
JAN 27'65	1,240			200.00 -		
JAN 27'65	41			100.00 -		
JAN 27'65	42			140.27 -		
JAN 29'65	43			41.62 -		3,370.29 ●
FEB 1'65	1,244			100.00 -		
FEB 11'65	45			6.38 -		
F '3'65	46			50.00 -		

MAVERICK CLARKE OF TEXAS   FORWARD

Exhibit 6-2—Machine Posted Ledger Sheet

MISCELLANEOUS JOURNAL ENTRIES

DATE	DESCRIPTION	NO.	DEBITS		CREDITS	
June	Insurance	106 ✓	538	77		
	Prepd ins	13 ✓			538	77
	To post 3 mo.					
June	Interest	116 ✓	56	90		
	Prepd interest	14 ✓			56	90
	To post 3 mo.					
June	Depn	114 ✓	375	00		
	"	103 ✓	666	36		
	Cell for Depn	3, R 3, R acts			666 375	36 00
	To post 3 mo.					
June	Accts Payable	50 ✓	3287	56	4650	66
	Fuel	104 ✓	697	52	958	57
	Ice	105 ✓	495	14	122	63
	Repairs	110 ✓	1279	49	827	83
	Rent	107 ✓	1168	64	714	86
	Supplies	112 ✓	263	25	369	75
	Transmitter	33 ✓	146	06	146	06
	Telephone	121 ✓	77	90	16	89
	Auto	113 ✓	266	37	3	55
	Legal & Acct	117 ✓	202	00	127	00
	Misc.	118 ✓	3	64		42
	To set up a/c payable					
	To reverse " "					

Exhibit 6-3—Miscellaneous Journal Entries

MISCELLANEOUS JOURNAL ENTRIES

DATE	DESCRIPTION	NO.	DEBITS		CREDITS	
June	Payroll taxes	120	52	71		
	Payroll taxes accrued	54			52	71
	To post 2 nd qtr					
Dec	Prepd insurance	170	2252	00		
	Prepd interest	171	92	00		
	Note payable	451			2344	00
	To post note payable – insurance				–	
	$293.00 a mo. start 8-21-65					
Oct	Social Security	422	38	00		
	Withholding	424	87	00		
	SS & W+				125	00
	To post 3 rd qtr.					
Dec	Insurance	925	359	10		
	Prepaid ins	170			359	10
	To post July – August					
Dec.	Insurance	925	750	64		
	Prepaid ins	170			750	64
	To post Sept Oct Nov & Dec					
					95	82
Dec	Interest	929	~~107 32~~ 95 82			
	Prepaid interest	171			~~107 32~~ 95 82	

Exhibit 6-3—Misscellaneous Journal Entries (continued)

TEXAS HARDWARE COMPANY			BEG BAL	THIS PERIOD	YEAR TO DATE
GENERAL LEDGER TRIAL BALANCE					
MAY 31, 1972				*	
1000001 CASH ON HAND BROWNSVILLE			410.00		:
1000001*				*	410.00
1000002 CASH ON HAND-LAREDO			780.00		
1000002*				*	780.00
1000003 CASH ON HAND-PHARR			200.00		
1000003*				*	200.00
1000004 CASH ON HAND-HARLINGEN					
100 4	5-31-2	JE17		150.00	
1000004*				150.00 *	150.00
1050000 1ST NATIONAL BANK-BROWNSVILLE			1,728.20		
105	5-31-2	JE14		13,016.92	
105	5-31-2	JE14		11,630.22-	
1050000*				1,386.70 *	3,114.90
1060000 LAREDO NATIONAL BANK			3,832.94		
106	5-31-2	JE15		14,508.32	
106	5-31-2	JE15		16,078.73-	
1060000*				1,570.41-*	2,262.53
1070000 SECURITY STATE BANK-PHARR			2,447.59		
107	5-31-2	JE16		2,076.32	
107	5-31-2	JE16		3,033.79-	
1070000*				957.47-*	1,490.12
1080000 1ST NATIONAL BANK-HARLINGEN			61.03		
108	5-31-2	JE17		8,437.98	
108	5-31-2	JE17		7,759.94-	
1080000*				678.04 *	739.07
1120000 TRANSFER OF FUNDS					
112	5-31-2	JE15		5,500.00	
112	5-31-2	JE16		1,500.00	
112	5-31-2	JE14		1,500.00-	
112	5-31-2	JE17		5,500.00-	
1120000*				*	
1310000 RETURN CHECKS			196.51		
1310000*				*	196.51
1320000 ACCT REC-EMPLOYEES			25.00		
132	5-31-2	JE17		65.12	
132	5-31-2	JE17		85.00-	
1320000*				19.88-*	5.12
1360000 ADVANCES TO OFFICERS			14,255.81		
1360000*				*	14,255.81
1500001 INVENTORY - BROWNSVILLE			36,523.02		
1500001*				*	36,523.02
1500002 INVENTORY - LAREDO			23,536.57		
1500002*				*	23,536.57
1500003 INVENTORY - PHARR			10,764.08		
1500003*				*	10,764.08
2070001 FURNITURE & FIXTURES-BRO			4,845.50		
2070001*				*	4,845.50
2070002 FURNITURE & FIXTURES-LAREDO			14,513.14		
2070002*				*	14,513.14
2070004 FURNITURE & FIXTURE HARLINGEN			150.00		
207 4	5-31-2	JE17		4,368.08	
2070004*				4,368.08 *	4,518.08
2100000 AUTO & TRUCKS			6,647.92		
2100000*				*	6,647.92
2110001 AIR CONDITIONING EQUIPMENT			1,723.57		
2110001*				*	1,723.57
				49,622.74	
62			122 640 88	45,587.68-	126,675.94

Exhibit 6-4—Trial Balance, Data Processing Equipment

SOUTHERN SHRIMP COMPANY
STATEMENT OF OPERATIONS
FOR 10 MONTHS ENDING MAY 31, 1972

	CURRENT MONTH	YEAR TO DATE 1972	YEAR TO DATE 1971
SALES	$ 15 562.84	$ 192 466.51	$ 108 683.80
FISHING AND PROCESSING EXPENSES			
CREW SHARE	5 050.23	65 057.96	37 006.09
GUARD SERVICE	14.00	140.00	112.00
ICE	277.88	3 591.39	1 893.27
CREW GROCERIES	810.17	5 422.55	3 767.14
PAYROLL TAXES	262.61	4 505.50	1 666.36
FUEL	2 541.41	12 684.77	13 338.05
SUPPLIES	1 641.75	11 542.33	11 385.81
NETS	181.00	955.55	1 058.50
REPAIRS	738.67	4 475.92	2 974.33
PROCESSING	5.85	2 068.48	303.52
TAXES & LICENCES	.00	290.77	373.27
DEPRECIATION	1 664.57	16 645.70	16 365.40
INSURANCE	4 250.00	9 100.00	4 950.00
INTEREST	415.62	4 550.70	5 602.83
	$ 17 853.76	$ 141 031.62	$ 100 886.57
FISHING PROFIT	$ 2 290.92-	$ 51 434.89	$ 7 797.23
OTHER EXPENSES			
BAD DEBTS	$ .00	$ 7.00	$ .00
DONATIONS	.00	12.50	12.50
DEPRECIATION-OTHER	.00	23.26	711.90
DUES,DONATIONS & SUBSCRIPTIONS	.00	130.88	166.00
LEGAL AND ACCOUNTING	50.00	530.12	903.06
LEASE EXPENSE	.00	2 137.50	2 137.50
MISCELLANEOUS	.00	.00	50.00
OFFICE SUPPLIES	13.44	13.44	.00
TAXES & LICENSES	.00	47.63	65.24
TRAVEL AND ENTERTAINMENT	.00	.00	367.35
	$ 63.44	$ 2 902.33	$ 4 413.55
PROFIT FOR THE PERIOD	$ 2 354.36-	$ 48 532.56	$ 3 383.68
RENTAL INCOME	.00	750.00	1 500.00
NET PROFIT	$ 2 354.36-	$ 49 282.56	$ 4 883.68

PREPARED WITHOUT AUDIT

Exhibit 6-5—Financial Statement Prepared by Data Processing Equipment

VALLEY WHOLESALE, INC.
STATEMENT OF FINANCIAL POSITION

LINE NO.		(1) 1-31-x2	(2) 2-28-x2	(3) 3-31-x2	(4) 4-30-x2	LINE NO.
	ASSETS					
1	Cash on hand and on deposit	$ 3589	$ 4011	$ 788	$ 3148	1
2	Accounts receivable, trade	80891	78471	87454	89667	2
3	Accounts receivable, returned checks	34	70	42	97	3
4	Merchandise inventory	89889	137643	144804	113178	4
5	Prepaid insurance	174	174	174	174	5
6	TOTAL CURRENT ASSETS	$ 174573	$ 770637	$ 711056	$ 706770	6
7						7
8	Property and Equipment					8
9	Store fixtures and equipment	$ 10876	$ 10876	$ 10876	$ 10876	9
10	Vehicles	7145	7145	7145	7145	10
11	Allowance for depreciation	⟨ 3848 ⟩	⟨ 4048 ⟩	⟨ 4248 ⟩	⟨ 4448 ⟩	11
12		$ 9173	$ 8973	$ 8773	$ 8573	12
13						13
14	Other Assets					14
15	Utility deposits	$ 33	$ 33	$ 33	$ 33	15
16	Organization expense	535	535	535	535	16
17		$ 568	$ 568	$ 568	$ 568	17
18		$ 184264	$ 779858	$ 770347	$ 715361	18
19						19
20	LIABILITIES					20
21	Accounts payable	$ 18781	$ 48904	$ 31687	$ 30383	21
22	Payroll taxes payable	1115	1375	1475	1353	22
23	Sales tax payable	1714	3743	5496	1939	23
24	Accrued corporation income tax	883	883	468	468	24
25	Accrued interest payable	—0—	44	160	777	25
26	Accrued property taxes	140	780	470	560	26
27	Accrued salaries	6333	5000	4500	4000	27
28	Note payable, Pan American Bank	—0—	15000	70000	70000	28
29	TOTAL CURRENT LIABILITIES	$ 28466	$ 74729	$ 64156	$ 58980	29
30						30
31	STOCKHOLDERS' EQUITY					31
32	Capital stock	$ 150000	$ 150000	$ 150000	$ 150000	32
33	Additional paid in capital	371	371	371	371	33
34	Retained Earnings:					34
35	Balance beginning of year	3716	3716	3716	3716	35
36	Net Profit for the period	7761	1594	2654	2844	36
37		$ 155798	$ 155729	$ 156191	$ 156381	37
38		$ 184264	$ 779858	$ 770347	$ 715361	38
39						39
40						40
41						41

Exhibit 6-6—Trend Type Financial Statement

STATISTICS 19X5-19X6

EXHIBIT "C"		MONTH		OF	
		JANUARY 19X6	FEBRUARY 19X6	MARCH 19X6	APRIL 19X6
INCOME STATEMENT COMPARISONS:					
NET SALES	- 19X6 Actual	30,741	25,648	25,258	21,621
	- 19X6 Budget	30,741	26,000	32,000	25,000
	- 19X5 Actual	29,947	26,922	32,091	24,899
GROSS PROFIT FROM SALES	- 19X6 Actual	8,377	6,989	6,891	5,892
	- 19X6 Budget	8,377	7,085	8,720	6,813
	- 19X5 Actual	8,385	7,538	8,985	6,972
EXPENSES	- 19X6 Actual	9,825	8,675	8,735	8,453
	- 19X6 Budget	9,825	8,809	10,203	9,484
	- 19X5 Actual	8,738	9,418	8,463	8,096
NET INCOME OR (LOSS) BEFORE TAXES	- 19X6 Actual	(2,176)	(1,609)	(1,907)	(2,676)
	- 19X6 Budget	(2,176)	(1,674)	(1,553)	(2,771)
	- 19X5 Actual	(423)	(1,713)	453	(1,229)
RATIO TO NET SALES	- 19X6 ACTUAL				
Total cost of sales		72.8 %	72.7 %	72.7 %	72.7 %
Officers' salaries		9.7 %	10.9 %	12.7 %	13.6 %
Payroll		6.4 %	6.7 %	7.2 %	7.5 %
Salesmen's commissions		7.5 %	7.5 %	7.0 %	5.1 %
All other expenses		8.3 %	8.7 %	7.6 %	12.9 %
Net other (income) or charges		2.4 %	(.3)%	.3 %	.5 %
Net income or (loss)		(7.1)%	(6.2)%	(7.5)%	(12.3)%
		100.0 %	100.0 %	100.0 %	100.0 %
BALANCE SHEET COMPARISON:					
CASH	- 19X6 Actual	11,865	10,621	10,640	9,569
	- 19X5 Acual	20,161	10,699	7,472	9,733
ACCOUNTS RECEIVABLE	- 19X6 Actual	62,758	58,227	48,164	44,728
	- 19X5 Actual	56,670	55,081	54,109	45,998
INVENTORIES	- 19X6 Actual	29,997	34,689	30,795	30,690
	- 19X5 Actual	37,513	40,170	36,995	32,630
NOTES PAYABLE	- 19X6 Actual	-	-	-	-
	- 19X5 Actual	-	-	-	-
ACCOUNTS PAYABLE	- 19X6 Actual	23,365	24,496	14,105	14,565
	- 19X5 Actual	32,352	27,078	19,573	13,743

Exhibit 6-7—Trend Statement

			YEAR	TO	DATE		
MAY 19X6	JUNE 19X6		2 MONTHS 2/28/X6	3 MONTHS 3/31/X6	4 MONTHS 4/30/X6	5 MONTHS 5/31/X6	6 MONTHS 6/30/X6
20,591	24,432		56,389	81,647	103,268	123,859	148,291
25,000	25,000		56,741	88,741	113,741	138,741	163,741
25,040	22,289		56,869	88,960	113,859	138,899	161,188
5,611	6,658		15,366	22,257	28,149	33,760	40,418
6,813	6,813		15,462	24,182	30,995	37,808	44,621
7,011	6,241		15,923	24,908	31,880	38,891	45,132
8,098	9,826		18,500	27,235	35,688	43,786	53,612
8,020	9,472		18,634	28,837	38,321	47,341	56,813
7,739	7,971		18,156	26,619	34,715	42,454	50,415
(3,015)	(3,214)		(3,785)	(5,692)	(8,368)	(11,383)	(14,597)
(2,307)	(2,609)		(3,850)	(5,403)	(8,174)	(10,481)	(13,090)
(838)	(1,683)		(2,136)	(1,683)	(2,912)	(3,750)	(5,433)
72.7 %	72.7 %		72.7 %	72.7 %	72.7 %	72.7 %	72.7 %
14.9 %	12.6 %		10.3 %	11.0 %	11.6 %	12.1 %	12.2 %
8.3 %	7.5 %		6.5 %	6.6 %	6.9 %	6.8 %	6.8 %
6.5 %	6.6 %		7.5 %	7.4 %	6.9 %	7.1 %	7.2 %
9.6 %	13.6 %		8.5 %	8.2 %	9.2 %	9.3 %	10.0 %
2.6 %	.2 %		1.2 %	.8 %	.8 %	1.1 %	.9 %
(14.6)%	(13.2)%		(6.7)%	(8.1)%	(8.1)%	(9.1)%	(9.8)%
100.0 %	100.0 %		100.0 %	100.0 %	100.0 %	100.0 %	100.0 %
9,195	4,588						
12,940	6,863						
42,356	46,857						
45,716	43,087						
31,233*	74,349						
41,200*	55,513						
-	-						
-	-						
15,373	63,048						
27,062	36,211						

Exhibit 6-7–Trend Statement (continued)

Dear Mr. Trapp:

This letter is written to outline the nature of the services we will be
performing for you and the financial arrangements for the work.

Our work will generally consist of performing the following services for you:

1. We will perform bookkeeping services consisting of preparation
    of journals, ledgers, employee earning records and the like
    that will be used in preparing financial statements and tax
    returns.
2. We will prepare financial statements monthly.
3. We will prepare quarterly payroll tax, sales tax and occupancy
    tax reports.
4. We will provide you with information regarding your business
    to be used in the preparation of your personal income tax
    return and will prepare your return, if you wish.

The financial statements will be prepared without audit and will be marked
"unaudited". The work we will be performing will be accounting service and
not audit service, and we will not express an auditor's opinion on the
financial statements. Our work is not designed to disclose defalcations or
irregularities in your operation, although their discovery may result.

The charges for our work will be based upon the amount of time spent and
calculated at our regular billing rates. Our rates vary from person to
person according to the degree of responsibility involved and skill required.

As I told you previously, I anticipate that the charges for these services
would be not more than $300.00 per month on the average. This will vary from
month to month depending on circumstances. It is likely that the first month
or two will have somewhat higher than average charges due to the effort
involved in getting the books set and the work organized, including computa-
tion of depreciation, etc. In future months, the quarterly report months
may run higher than average whereas the other two months of the quarter may
run below average. We will bill monthly for work performed.

It will definitely be to your advantage to do anything you can to reduce the
amount of work performed by us. We will be making suggestions to you from
time to time along this line.

We are very pleased to have the opportunity to serve you and look forward to
a pleasant relationship. We wish you well in your new venture and assure you
that your affairs will have our most careful attention at all times.

                        Very truly yours,

                 Exhibit 6-8—Engagement Letter for Bookkeeping Client

CHAPTER **7**

Auditing Small Companies:
Tested Practices and Procedures

The possibilities for performing audits for small clients are often over-looked; too many accountants think the small client either doesn't need an audit or can't afford one. The alert practitioner, however, will develop a "feel" for clients who should have an audit. Further, he must perform a quality job at a reasonable cost and furnish a report containing useful ideas and information.

Need for Audits by Small Clients

Keep this in mind about an audit; clients don't decide to spend hard-earned money for this service unless they are convinced they need it. The client frequently is not aware of the need nor or the advantages. Here are some advantages the accountant can point to:

1. An audit keeps the client's personnel (including the client himself) on their toes.
2. An audit provides an opportunity to locate and point out loose procedures and wasteful practices.
3. An audit frequently results in suggestions that save the client time and money.
4. An audit usually brings recommendations that strengthen the company's controls.
5. An audit provides assurance to the client, outside investors, creditors, and the public that the financial statements are fairly presented.
6. An audit is a plus factor in case of an IRS examination.

Audits are often considered to be a necessity where outside funds are either loaned or invested in the business. When you do an audit that has been requested because of outside interests, try to make your work so useful that the client will want you to continue an annual audit even if the outside influence is removed.

All organizations responsible to the public, either governmental, charitable, or civic in nature, should have an audit to check on stewardship of public funds. Such organizations include cities, school districts, water districts, churches, various civic clubs, etc. Furthermore, federal and state governments are channeling funds into local organizations and are requiring that the local agency report to them through an audit.

It is well to note that it is also in the best interest of the accountant to perform an audit wherever possible. The public, clients and the courts do not always have a clear understanding of the difference between audited and unaudited statements, and the liability exposure from preparation of unauditied statements is clearly growing. Accountants run the risk of liability exposure with regard to non-audit clients for errors, omissions or defalcations even though the accountant clearly has no responsibility for detection. There is considerable responsibility and exposure in connection with audit work, but the accountant's audit procedures substantially reduce the risk of errors.

Is the Client "Auditable"?

The small client occasionally presents a unique problem; his accounting records are in such poor condition they can't be audited (or can be audited only after extensive straightening out). It is generally undesirable to undertake an audit of records that are obviously inferior; the time consumed can be excessive, the job frustrating and the cost expensive.

In these circumstances, several alternative approaches should be considered:

1. Ask the client to make arrangements to get the books straightened out under your supervision before you start the audit.
2. If you are to do all the work involving straightening out the books, be sure the client understands the problem and agrees to the cost involved.
3. It may be that the best approach is to suggest that the audit be postponed for a year and the first assignment be to set up a good accounting system and adequate controls. This is a constructive approach to the problem and avoids an expensive audit of poor records.

Reaching an Understanding with the Client

In audit engagements, more than any other type of accounting work, you need a clear understanding with the client. The understanding should cover the nature of the work to be performed and the fee arrangement. It should be set forth in writing in the form of an engagement letter. Such a letter is found in Exhibit 7-1.

The accountant should fully discuss with the client the nature of the audit and its purpose. The average layman has little understanding of this point. Historically, audits have been widely publicized whenever a shortage of public funds was found and most people think locating embezzlements is the primary function of an audit. On the other hand, they have very little understanding of the meaning of the accountant's opinion on the financial statements. The client needs to be clearly advised that audits are not designed to discover embezzlements, although they frequently do so, and surely prevent many more. Clients should be informed that it is more economical to protect against embezzlement through the use of fidelity bonds and a good system of internal control.

Our firm has tried to explain some of these points through the use of a client bulletin. This bulletin is found in Exhibit 7-2 and may provide the reader with suggestions to be used in discussing or writing to clients on this subject.

Need for Top Quality Performance

The accountant has a special responsibility for quality performance in audit work. The examination of, and reporting on, financial statements is the one field reserved exclusively for the accountant. The profession has well defined standards to be followed and abundant literature explaining the auditor's responsibilities. Every audit engagement, no matter how small, should be performed with care. A written audit program should be prepared prior to the commencing of the work and adequate work papers should document the audit procedures and findings.

It is well worth mentioning at this point that the practitioner should carry adequate liability insurance. The discovery of a significant error in financial statements upon which the accountant has expressed his opinion exposes him to considerable financial risk. Third parties who have lost money because of placing reliance on erroneous financial statements frequently file law suits against the accountant for recovery of damages. There are two ways to overcome this problem: (1) perform a first-class audit and (2) carry plenty of liability insurance.

Where to Do the Work

In auditing small businesses and public organizations, it is sometimes difficult to decide whether to work in your office or the client's office. It is best to perform the audit in the client's office, if at all possible. Here is the most convient place to work with the client's records and personnel. Here you will be able to concentrate on the audit without the interruptions encountered in your own office. The work done in the client's office should carry the audit through its completion, including the writing of the audit report. There is a temptation to come back to your office and write the report after completing the field work. Frequently, however, the writing of the report requires you to look up additional information which is available only in the client's office.

On the other hand, it is sometimes necessary to have the books and supporting data sent to your office and the audit work performed there. Some of the smaller civic and charitable organizations have office facilities that are so limited that you simply cannot work there. In your office, you have the advantage of a suitable and familiar place to work. If the client can't provide an adequate desk and lighting, it is probably best to take the material to your office.

Doing the Job at a Reasonable Cost

It takes time and effort to perform a good audit; keeping the cost under control is a real problem. You have to be able to do the job at a fee that is acceptable to the client. Experienced accountants approach this problem from two angles; first, make the audit so useful that the client will feel it is fully worth the price and second, use all the time-saving techniques you can devise.

A very effective method of cutting down time is to have the client prepare all essential supporting data such as schedules, analyses and working trial balances. The client should clearly understand that assistance on his part will help hold down the cost of the audit. He and his staff should be requested to be of as much assistance as they possibly can. The firm of Sartain, Fischbein, Kurtz & Company of Tulsa, Oklahoma, has devised an engagement letter (Exhibit 7-3) which clearly outlines the items the client is to furnish. The use of such a letter would certainly facilitate an understanding with the client on this important point.

One word of caution: don't let the client's personnel do work that constitutes part of the audit itself. The schedules prepared by the client must be carefully checked and all their work fully verified. The items they are asked to do must be selected with care.

Care also must be exercised so that others do not get the impression you are letting the client's personnel do more work than they should. The writer encountered a problem in this area several years ago. I was planning to visit the branch of a client for the purpose of auditing the branch. The client's controller wanted to review the work at the branch, also. It was decided that the controller should accompany me and perform some limited, routine audit procedures, which would be of help to both of us. This came to the attention of a large creditor of the client, who objected to the fact that I was not doing an "independent" audit.

There are numerous ways the auditor can save his own time in the performance of his work. Bear in mind that much time is consumed in the physical preparation of work papers, copying of trial balances, depreciation schedules, account analyses, and the like. Look for ways to cut down on this time. Here are a few suggestions:

1. Rather than preparing a bank reconciliation yourself, make a photo copy of the client's reconciliation and check it.
2. Use your copying machine to duplicate such items as the account headings from last year's working trial balance, depreciation schedules, and the like.
3. When analyzing an account make a copy of the client's ledger sheet to avoid rewriting information already there.
4. Obtain rubber stamps for use in certain repetitive items such as the client's name, dates and headings. Some rubber stamps can be used on many different audits.
5. Use standard confirmation forms designed so that only a limited amount of material must be physically filled in (See Exhibit 7-4 as an example of an accounts receivable confirmation form wherein both the confirmation request and the reply are on the same page.)

Review of Internal Control

One of the auditing standards to which the practitioner must adhere is as follows:

> There is to be a proper study and evaluation of the existing internal control as a basis for reliance thereon and for the determination of the resultant extent of the tests to which auditing procedures are to be restricted.

Some auditors assume that there can be little or no internal control in the small company, hence they disregard this facet of the audit. Every company, however, has certain elements of internal control and the auditor can educate the client in ways to strengthen what they already have. Internal control involves not only safeguards to minimize errors and the risk of fraud, but also such areas as a clear definition of duties and responsibilities, proper utilization of personnel and the system of accounting and reporting. Budgeting is an internal control feature if a budget is in use. Management should be vitally interested in internal control regardless of the size of the business.

The system of internal control is a key factor in the cost of the audit. Without adequate internal control a more detailed examination must be made, hence increasing the time and cost involved. The auditor must rely on proper internal control in order to know the extent of testing and sampling he should do in the performance of the work.

One of the problems often encountered in the small organization is the office with only one person. Here there can be no division of duties as in the larger company. Offsetting this, however, is something as good or perhaps even better: an alert and interested owner. Actually, the smaller the business, the more internal control is usually exercised by the owner himself. This is for his benefit and the auditor can frequently suggest more effective ways for the owner to exercise control.

The auditor for the small client must evaluate the owner's ability to provide control. He should ask himself: does the owner know how to exercise control? Is he personally inclined to perform such tasks as opening the mail? Is he really interested in a well organized and controlled operation?

The auditor may have a selling job to do, especially if changes are indicated. The owner may not want to offend long-time employees. The whole concept of internal control may sound like an idea for a large company, but nevertheless, the owner can play a vital role in this area.

The review of internal control should be conducted at the outset of the audit. It is here that the information is gathered and decisions made as to the extent of auditing tests that are necessary. Internal control review performed toward the end of an audit is much less effective than that done at the beginning.

Internal control questionnaires are very helpful in performing this review. Our firm has a "short form" questionnaire that can be used for smaller clients (Exhibit 7-5). This questionnaire highlights the controls that can be helpful in the smaller business, including the part played by the owner.

Reporting on the Audit

The auditor's report should convey useful knowledge and ideas to the client and to other readers. Chapter 4 covered this subject, giving examples of financial statements, presentation and comments, (see Exhibits 4-4 and 4-5).

The auditor is responsible for complying with the reporting standards of the profession. He will have to decide the type of opinion he will render on the financial statements. The four types of opinions an auditor can render are as follows:

1. An unqualified opinion, sometimes called a "clean" opinion.
2. A qualified opinion, wherein exceptions are taken to certain items which are not sufficiently material to require a disclaimer of opinion of the financial statements as a whole.
3. A disclaimer, wherein the auditor states that he cannot express his opinions of the statements. This normally results from such problems as restrictions on the amount of audit work to be done, inadequate records or internal control, or some material exception to the accounting principles being used by the client.
4. An adverse opinion, wherein the auditor states that the financial statements are not presented in accordance with generally accepted principles of accounting. This latter opinion is used rarely, since neither the client nor the auditor wants to make such a statement. Usually, the problems that require such an opinion are corrected before the financial statement is issued.

Professional standards also require that certain types of information about the accounting policies of the client, contingent liabilities and the like be disclosed. The practitioner must be well-versed and up to date on professional pronouncements in this area.

The Management Letter

In addition to the auditor's report, the client should be given a letter commenting on matters that came to the auditor's attention during the audit. This letter can be more informal than the report itself and can range over a wide variety of subjects. It is intended for the client's internal use and can speak frankly of problems that would not normally be mentioned in the audit report, which is often given to outsiders.

It is in the management letter that the auditor can tell the client of deficiencies in his accounting system, internal control, problems with heavy expenses or large inventories and the like. The management letter is not limited to accounting matters, either, as the auditor should be alert and observant while in the client's place of business and comment on any item that he feels could be improved upon.

Do not minimize the importance of the letter by enumerating petty items along with serious weaknesses. For example, an auditor commenting on a three-dollar shortage in the petty cash fund would distract from the more important comment that the cashier had not taken a vacation in six years.

If there are numerous comments on a variety of subjects, the letter should be broken down into different categories. Those comments regarding accounting and bookkeeping matters, for instance, should be separated from others of a general management nature. In management letters to larger clients, the comments are frequently presented on a departmental basis so that heads of different departments will readily locate those that apply to them. This same principle can apply in some circumstances to the letter to a smaller client.

The auditor may have recommendations which he realizes the client will have difficulty in following. If the recommendation is sound, however, the auditor should go on record with it. Furthermore, certain recommendations should be repeated in subsequent letters from year to year. It is best to be fully on record concerning a potential problem; if not, you may be in trouble later.

The effectiveness of the management letter is limited only by the practitioner's powers of observation and ability to come up with useful recommendations. There is no standard form to be used, but Exhibit 7-6 provides an example of one approach.

Reporting to the Board of Directors

In the case of a civic, charitable, or governmental client, you may be requested to report to the board of directors. Here is an occasion to sell yourself effectively; or to create a negative impression. Be fully prepared for the meeting. Be sure you speak with knowledge and authority. Review the financial statements so that you highlight the type of information discussed in Chapter 4. The management letter and its recommendations should also be discussed.

Learn to communicate with the directors in an understandable manner. Avoid the use of technical accounting jargon and explain your material clearly. An overhead projector is useful in such meetings, since the material under discussion can be projected onto a screen. This insures that everyone is discussing the same data. In the absence of an overhead projector, refer to certain pages of the audit report and have sufficient copies so that everyone has his own.

This is also an opportunity to explain the function and the responsibility of the auditor. These items should have been mentioned and clarified in the engagement letter, but bringing them up in the board of directors' meeting makes it certain that all present have gotten the message. Also, in the case of a client of long standing, you may have discontinued using an engagement letter each year and this would be an occasion to remind the board of your function.

Special Audit Problems When You Have Kept Books

You may be requested to audit a client for whom you have kept the books. Such a request might come from a bank or other creditor, or from the stockholders if they are not active in the management of the business.

Are You Independent?—One problem that must be resolved in such an event is the question of your independence. An auditor must have certain attributes of independence: he must not have a financial interest in the company, he must not be an employee of the company or in any other way have been associated with the client in a manner that would impair his objectivity in performing and reporting on the audit.

Professional accounting literature contains some material on the question of independence when auditing a bookkeeping client. The consensus is that independence is not impaired, assuming that the client is only one of a number served. While none of the committees of the American Institute of Certified Public Accountants have ever issued a formal statement on this subject, the views stated above have been aired in *The Journal of Accountancy,* and presumably represent the informal thinking of the appropriate committees.

The Audit Program—In undertaking an audit where he has kept the books, the accountant should give serious thought to the audit program. He may have a more difficult time deciding on his audit procedures than if someone else had kept the books. He may feel that where he has kept the books some of the normal procedures could be omitted. In short, he has been so close to the bookkeeping work that he may not be able to "see the forest for the trees."

Auditing Procedures—There are some auditing procedures that are always undertaken, such as observation of the physical inventory, the confirmation of accounts receivable, bank balances, and notes payable by direct correspondence, etc.

On the other hand, it would seem that testing the postings of journals and ledgers, testing of addition and certain similar steps could be reduced in scope or possibly eliminated.

Internal Control—A review of the client's system of internal control should be made as usual. This would encompass such points as reviewing the system for handling incoming cash, control of sales invoices and other documents, approving and paying bills, etc. This review would require visiting the place of business and observing procedures first hand.

Where to Work—In making an audit of this type, the accountant would probably perform quite a bit of the work in his office, since the books would normally be there already. This, of course, is different from the usual procedure of conducting an audit in the client's place of business. There might be a psychological advantage in taking the books to the client's office and doing the work there. Such a step would create the actual atmosphere of an audit and would help dispel any feeling of complacency in the mind of the practitioner.

The Audit Report—The question arises whether it should be disclosed in the audit report that the auditor has kept the books. This is one that each practitioner must decide in the circumstances. Points to be considered in making such a decision include the reason the audit was originally requested, and the persons to whom the report is going.

Importance of First-Class Appearance

Your audit work will be judged to a large extent by its appearance. Even though you have put in many hours of work and done a quality audit, the client receives only the audit report as the finished product. Your product should have a professional appearance in every respect. Each copy should be uniform in appearance and show no evidence of erasures. The report paper should be of high professional quality. The format of the financial statements should be readable and informative. The statements and comments in Exhibits 4-4 and 4-5 are presented as examples of a professional product.

Using the Audit to Sell Additional Work

An audit provides an opportunity to delve into the client's transactions and system in depth. It will reveal problems and deficiencies that should be commented on in the management letter. At this point, the auditor should advise the client of his ability to be of assistance in correcting some of the problems enumerated. These might fall in the area of improving the accounting system, advance planning on tax problems, financial budgeting and forecasting, assistance in obtaining additional needed financing, or a multitude of areas within the framework of general management. Many ideas are set forth in the succeeding chapters of this book for additional clients' services which may be brought to light by the audit.

Conclusion

There are many opportunities to provide a useful service to small clients by performing an audit. Learn to recognize when a client needs an audit. Keep up to date on professional standards and develop your techniques for saving time (and don't hesitate to learn all you can from others). And bear in mind that auditing is high-level professional service. A well-done audit report can do much for your professional reputation.

Mr. George Allen, President
Southwest Manufacturing Company
Brownsville, Texas

Dear Mr. Allen:

We are pleased that you have employed this firm to perform an audit of your
company for the year ending September 30, 19X7. This letter is for the
purpose of discussing the nature of our services and the method of determining our charges.

We will perform an examination of your financial statements in accordance
with generally accepted auditing standards. This will include a review of
your system of internal control, as well as tests of transactions and of
your accounting records to the extent we believe necessary. We will observe
your physical inventory and make independent confirmations of your receivables,
payables and certain other items.

This examination is for the purpose of enabling us to express our professional
opinion on your financial statements. We do not plan to make a detailed examination of all transactions, nor is our audit designed to disclose defalcations
or other irregularities. This discovery may result, but this cannot be assured.

Based upon the present size and scope of activities of your company, we estimate our fee for this examination will not exceed $3,500.00. Our charges are
based on the amount of time required to perform the work, and cannot be determined precisely in advance. Should any unforeseen problems arise during the
examination that would change our estimated fee, we will notify you immediately.

We are pleased at the opportunity to be of service to you, and will give this
work our most careful attention. If the foregoing arrangements are acceptable
to you, will you please sign the enclosed copy of this letter in the space
provided and return it to us.

Exhibit 7-1—Audit Engagement Letter

LONG, CHILTON & COMPANY
CLIENT BULLETIN

We have had the rather painful experience in recent months of working in two
situations in which significant shortages of funds were uncovered. In both
instances public funds were involved and the situation received considerable
TV and newspaper coverage. As a result, we have received some comments and
questions about our participation in these audits. This newsletter, therefore,
will discuss some of the things we try to accomplish in an audit.

There seems to be a feeling on the part of some people that an auditor is
primarily a bloodhound engaged in tracking down embezzlers. The primary
purpose of the normal audit, however, is not that of uncovering defalcations
and embezzlements - - it is, rather, to enable the auditor to express his
professional opinion on the client's financial statements. An audit report
is frequently used by a variety of parties in addition to the client - -
credit grantors, governmental agencies, bonding companies, etc. The most
useful function of an audit is to assure that the financial statements are
properly presented, and work performed is directed toward that end. Such
auditing procedures, for instance, as direct confirmation of receivables and
payables and physical observation of inventories are primarily done to
determine that the various assets and liabilities are fairly stated.

While the normal audit is not primarily designed to discover embezzlements,
this is nevertheless a factor that is considered. Audits frequently do uncover
embezzlements, and more importantly, prevent many more. The auditor reviews
the client's internal procedures and makes recommendations when controls are
weak. Most embezzlements would never occur if the guilty party was not tempted
by weak controls. One of the important functions of an audit is to recommend
controls that will prevent someone from taking that first step toward an
embezzlement.

If auditors were to guarantee to discover every theft, the scope of the work
would have to be greatly increased. The cost would be prohibitive. Auditors
do not examine every transaction, but rely on testing and sampling and on
proper controls within the clients organization. It should also be borne in
mind that most companies continue to bond their employees, even though they
have audits. Bond coverage is an essential protection against employee dis-
honesty at a reasonable cost.

We are, naturally, firm believers in the value of an audit. It gives assurance
to owners, stockholders, bankers and others that the accounting records are
in order and the figures can be relied upon. There has been a trend in recent
years for more and more organizations to have audits, and this trend will
undoubtedly continue. We hope this article has clarified what can and cannot be expected from an audit.

Exhibit 7-2—Client Bulletin Discussing Audit Work

———————————————   ———————————————
                                                        (Date)
———————————————

———————————————

Dear_____

    In order for us to be more efficient in the examination of your company for the year ended_____, we recommend that you provide the following information prior to our beginning the field work.

_____The general ledger should be in balance and as correct as possible.

_____Prepared reconciliations for each bank account.

_____We will furnish bank confirmation forms to be filled in and signed.

_____Prepare a schedule of accounts receivable - trade, preferably showing how long the accounts have been carried.

_____We will furnish account receivable confirmations to be filled in and signed.

_____Prepare a schedule of accounts receivable, officers and employees.

_____Prepare a schedule of bad debts written off during the year.

_____Prepare a schedule of notes receivable. Also, have the notes available for our inspection.

_____Prepare a schedule of transactions for the period with affiliated enterprises.

_____Have the original inventory sheets ready for us after pricing and extending have been done.

_____Prepare an analysis of all transactions affecting marketable securities during the period.

_____Prepare a schedule of insurance showing the following: policy number, coverage, term and premium paid. Also, have the policies available for our inspection.

_____Prepare a schedule of all property and equipment additions and retirements showing cost and, for items sold, sales price.

_____Prepare a schedule of depreciation.

_____Prepare a schedule of the life insurance for officers, showing name of officer, insurance company, policy number, date issued, amount of coverage and annual premium.

_____Prepare a schedule of accounts payable. Also, save the creditor's regular monthly statements for _____ where available.
                                    (date)

_____Have copies of all payroll tax reports available to us.

_____Prepare a schedule of notes payable showing dates, payee, original balance, audit date balance, amount of periodic installment, rate of interest and describe security.

_____Have the corporate stock book and minute book brought up to date and available to us.

Exhibit 7-3—Letter Requesting Assistance from Client

————————————
————————————
(Date)

_____Prepare a schedule of all transactions to partners' capital and drawing accounts
for the period.

_____Have a copy of the partnership agreement available to us.

_____Have a copy of all leases for manufacturing or office space and equipment
rental contracts available to us.

_____Have a copy of any employment contracts with salesmen or executives available
to us.

_____Have a copy of pension/profit sharing agreement and letter of acceptance from
the Treasury Department available to us.

_____Schedule all repairs in excess of $_____.

_____Schedule each officer's salary and expense account payments.

_____Schedule all contributions.

_____Schedule all taxes paid.

_____Schedule all professional fees.

We understand that we are to make an examination of the financial statements of
_____as of_____
and to express our opinion on the statements. The examination is to be conducted in
accordance with generally accepted auditing standards and will include such tests
of the accounting records and such other auditing procedures as we may consider
necessary. It is not contemplated that we shall make a detailed examination of all
transactions, such as would be necessary to disclose any defalcations or irregularities which may have occurred.

Our charges for this examination will be at our usual per diem rates, plus any
direct out of pocket expenses that we incur.

We will inform you immediately of any auditing problems we encounter. Any
suggestions for improving the internal control or other items which we believe
feasible will be directed to your attention at the conclusion of the engagement.

Please call on us for any questions you have regarding the items mentioned in
this letter.

Very truly yours,

SARTAIN, FISCHBEIN, KURTZ & CO.

————————————
(Partner)

Exhibit 7-3–Letter Requesting Assistance from Client (Continued)

_____

_____

_____

Dear Sir:
    Sirs:

        For the purpose of obtaining independent confirmation of accounts receivable, we are asking customers to confirm the balances of their accounts with us as of_____ _____ direct to our accountants, Cheatham, Brady, Lafferty & Cox. In this connection we are enclosing a statement of your account to that date and, after comparing the statement with your records, we shall appreciate your signing the confirmation below and returning it to our accountants in the enclosed addressed envelope; in case the amounts are not in agreement with your records, please note your exceptions in the space provided therefor.

        This letter is not intended to be a request for payment of your account.

                         Yours very truly,

                   (Signed)_____

                            By:_____

CONFIRMATION OF ACCOUNTS RECEIVABLE

Cheatham, Brady, Lafferty & Cox
701 Shepherd Drive
P. O. Box 7886
Houston, Texas 7707

                         Reference _____

                         Number   _____

Dear Sirs:

        According to our records the balance of \$_____at_____ shown by the statement as owing by us is correct except as noted below: (Please list any charges you do not accept, credits you have not been allowed, or other differences showing dates and amounts).

                         Yours very truly,

                     (Signed) _____

                            BY: _____

Date_____, 19____.

Exhibit 7-4—Accounts Receivable Confirmation Request and Reply

INTERNAL CONTROL QUESTIONNAIRE
SHORT FORM

CLIENT_____ PERIOD ENDED_____

QUESTION	ANSWER YES NO N/A	REMARKS ("No answers require explanations.)
1. General		
a. Are accounting records kept up to date and balanced monthly?		
b. Is a chart of accounts used?		
c. Does the owner use a budget system for watching income and expenses?		
d. Are cash projections made?		
e. Are adequate monthly financial reports available to the owner?		
f. Does the owner appear to take a direct and active interest in the financial affairs and reports which should be or are available.		
g. Are the personal funds of the owner and his personal income and expenses completely segregated from the business?		
h. Is the owner satisfied that all employees are honest?		
i. Is the bookkeeper required to take annual vacations?		
2. Cash Receipts		
a. Does the owner open the mail?		
b. Does the owner list mail receipts before turning them over to the bookkeeper?		
c. Is the listing of the receipts subsequently traced to the cash receipts journal?		
d. Are the over-the-counter receipts controlled by cash register tapes, counter receipts, etc.?		
e. Are receipts deposited intact daily?		
f. Are employees who handle funds bonded?		
3. Cash Disbursements		
a. Are all disbursements made by check?		
b. Are prenumbered checks used?		
c. Is a controlled, mechanical check protector used?		
d. Is the owner's signature required on checks?		

Exhibit 7-5—Internal Questionnaire (Short Form)

SHORT FORM
INTERNAL CONTROL QUESTIONNAIRE (Continued)

QUESTION	YES	NO	N/A	REMARKS ("No answers require explanations.)
e. Does the owner sign checks only after they are properly completed? (Checks should not be signed in blank.)				
f. Does the owner approve and cancel the documentation in support of all disbursements?				
g. Are all voided checks retained and accounted for?				
h. Does the owner review the bank reconciliation?				
i. Is an imprest petty cash fund used?				
4. Accounts Receivable a. Are work order and/or sales invoices pre-numbered and controlled?				
b. Are customers' ledgers balanced regularly?				
c. Are monthly statements sent to all customers?				
d. Does the owner review statements before mailing?				
e. Are account write-offs and discounts approved only by the owner?				
f. Is credit granted only by the owner?				
5. Notes Receivable a. Does the owner have sole access to notes and investment certificates?				
6. Inventories a. Is the person responsible for inventory someone other than the bookkeeper?				
b. Are periodic physical inventories taken?				
c. Is there physical control over inventory stocks?				
d. Are perpetual inventory records maintained?				
7. Property Assets a. Are there detailed records available of property assets and allowances for depreciation?				
b. Is the owner acquainted with property assets owned by the company?				
c. Are retirements approved by the owner?				

Exhibit 7-5—Internal Questionnaire (Short Form) (continued)

SHORT FORM
INTERNAL CONTROL QUESTIONNAIRE (continued)

QUESTION	ANSWERS YES NO N/A	REMARKS ("No" answers require explanations.)
8. Accounts Payable and Purchases a. Are purchase orders used?		
b. Does someone other than the bookkeeper always do the purchasing?		
c. Are suppliers' monthly statements compared with recorded liabilities regularly?		
d. Are suppliers' monthly statements checked by the owner periodically if disbursements are made from invoice only?		
9. Payroll a. Are the employees hired by the owner?		
b. Would the owner be aware of the absence of any employee?		
c. Does the owner approve, sign, and distribute payroll checks?		
10. Brief Narrative of Auditor's Conclusion as to Adequacy of Internal Control.		

_____
_____
_____
_____
_____

Exhibit 7-5—Internal Questionnaire (Short Form) (continued)

Board of Directors
Southmost Construction Company
Brownsville, Texas

Gentlemen:

In connection with the audit of your company we reviewed various controls and procedures and have the following comments and recommendations:

MATERIALS IN SHOP YARD - The value of materials in the shop yard is not know but could amount to a sizeable sum. These materials are stored in the open without protection. We suggest that you consider having a sale to get rid of items that are not needed by the Company. You also should consider some type of fencing in order to provide more protection for the materials on hand.

EQUIPMENT LOCATED ON JOBS - You are now able to keep up reasonably well with equipment by personal contact with the jobs and knowledge of where equipment is located. As the Company grows, however, this will become more of a problem. In the future it may be necessary to set up procedures requiring that all movements of equipment be accounted for.

We understand that you do not want to burden the job superintendents with anymore paperwork than absolutely necessary. At the present time, therefore, we feel the control of equipment could be maintained reasonably well through the office by keeping the present equipment log complete and up to date.

RECEIPT OF MATERIAL AT JOB SITE - Looking again to future growth of the Company it may be necessary to establish additional controls in this area. Consideration should be given to requiring that certain personnel are designated to receive material on the job, that the material is checked as it is received and a pre-numbered receiving report be used.

PAYROLL CONTROL - The Company has now about 135 employees, which makes it impossible for anyone to know each employee. Procedures should be used, therefore, to provide a periodic check to see that all employees receiving checks are actually physically working for the company. This could be done by periodically having an officer distribute payroll checks for the week.

In connection with regular weekly payroll procedure the following should be observed:

Exhibit 7-6—Management Letter

1. The superintendent should deliver checks personally to the employees. This should not be assigned to someone else.

2. After checks have been signed they should not be returned to the person preparing the checks. The signer should deliver them to the job superintendent direct.

3. Superintendents should deliver unclaimed checks back to one of the officers with an explanation as to why it was unclaimed. It should not be turned back directly to the person preparing the checks.

EMPLOYEE LOANS - Accounting records for employee loans should be kept up to date at all times. A listing of loans outstanding should be prepared for the officers at least once a month.

DEPOSITING OF INCOMING CHECKS - In some instances certain types of income has been deposited directly to savings accounts. We recommend that this practice be discontinued and that all income be deposited into the Company's checking account. Transfer to savings accounts then can be made by check.

CANCELLATION OF PAID INVOICES - Invoices that have been paid should be so marked with a rubber stamp in order to prevent the possibility of paying them again. Paid invoices are now stapled to a copy of the check. We recommend, however, that they be clearly marked as having been paid.

JOB COST ACCOUNTING - Under the present system costs are charged to jobs based upon the issuance of a check. The material and the invoice have been received some two to five weeks prior to the writing of the check, however. We suggest that you consider revising your system so that the job is charged for a cost immediately upon receipt of the invoice. This will keep job cost records more up to date and provide more current and accurate information.

BOND COVERAGE - The Company now has no indemnity bond coverage on any employees. We feel it would be desirable to consider such coverage on the officers and the accounting personnel and suggest that this matter be investigated.

INTEREST EARNED AND PAID - Yield on cash investments could be improved in some instances by purchasing CD's. Also, interest is being paid on short term notes at higher rates than is being earned on funds invested. You should consider either cashing in or borrowing invested funds rather than paying current interest rates on short term funds.

We will be glad to discuss any of these comments in further detail if you wish.

Very truly yours,

Exhibit 7-6—Management Letter (continued)

CHAPTER 8

Improving the Small Client's Office and Accounting System

Thomas Edison is credited with the statement "There's a better way to do it, find it." This statement holds true for accounting systems. There are very few, if any, that can't be improved.

The accountant is in a position to detect a system's problems. He can then follow a few basic principles and do wonders for the client's office. This chapter covers these points as well as techniques for dealing with salesmen, helping the client with his accounting personnel and specific ways of saving time.

How to Recognize a Problem

There are certain points to watch for that indicate problems in an office. Here are a few:

1. Books always behind and financial statements late.
2. Office personnel and expense increasing faster than sales revenue.
3. Confusion among office personnel as to their duties and responsibilities.
4. Difficulty in keeping up to date with billing, paying bills and other normal office work.
5. Inability of management to get current information on cash, accounts receivable, accounts payable, etc.

Basic Requirements for the Accounting System

Most clients want two things from their accounting system; first, simplicity and ease of operation and second, full and complete information of all types at their fingertips. These two desires are obviously somewhat in conflict and there has to be some give and take on both points. One point to bear in mind, however; it is best to keep the system as simple as possible. Resist the temptation to make it overly complicated, especially in a small business. A simple system has these advantages: the client and his people can understand it better; it requires less time and expense to operate; it is easier to keep it up to date.

Another point to remember is the need for adequate internal controls. There are few clients who don't appreciate the need for controls. They are receptive to ideas that will help safeguard their assets and give them control over their operations.

Human Relations—Don't forget the human factor when suggesting changes in a system. People have a natural tendency to resist change. They prefer to stay with the familiar ways of doing things and, further, you may be trying to change a system or procedure they originated. Any time you suggest change, you imply that there is something wrong. Tact, diplomacy and salesmanship are necessary to overcome resistance.

Remember, too, that the owner of the business is entitled to his own idiosyncrasies. You will find instances where changes are desirable but cannot be implemented because the owner likes things the way they are. We have a client who for years has had his books set up with the debits on the right and the credits on the left. It has been suggested that his books be changed to conform with the normal arrangement, but he understands the present system and does not want to change. Under the circumstances, it would be pointless to make an issue of this item.

In Chapter 7, the subject of Internal Control for small companies was discussed and an internal control questionnaire was presented in Exhibit 7-5. Even though the client is not planning to have an audit, the material in Chapter 7 is fully applicable to the installation and review of accounting systems. Internal control is important to all clients—large or small, audit or otherwise.

A Review of a Small Client's Office

If a client is having problems, suggest that you do a survey of office procedures. The purpose is to get an overall view of how the office is operating. Don't go into great depth concerning all the ramifications of various problems but limit yourself to a general overall review. Concentrate only on the system and procedures. Don't become involved in discussions of income tax and other matters. By concentrating on this one area, you can cover the ground quickly. Frequently, a survey of this type will come up with a considerable number of valuable suggestions without the need for doing any further work. Problems may come up, of course, that will require additional services.

When you do systems work, it is essential to report to the client on what you have accomplished. Exhibit 8-1 is an example of a letter written to a client after conducting a survey of his system such as described in the preceeding paragraphs. An important feature is the highlighting of projected savings resulting from the various suggestions. This gives the client a basis for evaluating your recommendations. Further, it is more likely that he will appreciate the work you have done.

Helping the Client with Office Personnel

The accountant can be of great assistance in helping his clients locate and employ capable office personnel. He is generally better able to evaluate the qualifications of office personnel than is the client. Usually, the accountant knows where to find personnel as well as how to interview and test the qualifications of bookkeepers, secretaries, etc. Be careful, of course, not to make the final decision regarding employment, since this is the client's responsibility. The best procedure is for the accountant to assist in recruiting, interviewing, testing, checking references, evaluating qualifications, etc. It is best for the client to handle negotiations with the prospective employee regarding compensation, vacations, hours to be worked and the like.

Locating Personnel—Bookkeepers, secretaries and clerical personnel can generally best be located through the following sources:

1. Newspaper advertisements
2. Employment agencies
3. Local offices of the State Employment Commission

Advertising for personnel has the advantage of attracting applicants who might not otherwise apply. Not everyone who is available for a job registers with an employment office. Some people are dissatisfied with their present jobs but are not actively looking for new ones. Someone in this category often can be located through the use of an advertisement.

Most employers place "blind" ads rather than identify their names. When the employer uses his name, he runs the risk of having to respond to a large number of applicants, receiving telephone calls and offending those who are not employed. On the other hand, a blind ad has the disadvantage of discouraging someone who might otherwise apply. People who are presently employed are not as likely to respond to a blind ad.

When dealing with commercial employment agencies, remember that the prospective employee must pay a fee upon finding a job. In times of a tight labor market, employers sometimes offer to pay the fee themselves. In other instances, the employer advises the employee that 50 percent of the fee will be reimbursed after six months employment. Keep these incentives in mind when dealing with this situation.

Checking References—A prospective employee can be expected to provide only those references that are favorable. It is best, therefore, to check references by telephone. This usually brings a more spontaneous evaluation than would a letter. A great deal can be learned from the manner in which the reference speaks. The tone and inflection of voice identify an enthusiastic response, as opposed to one where the reference is hesitant. You are more likely to get adverse information over the telephone than in writing.

It is also possible to get information from people other than the applicant's own references. The employment application form should require the applicant to list each and every job held during the past several years. It is imperative that one or more former employers be contacted regarding the applicant's standing. Ask if the applicant would be eligible for re-employment. Be alert to determine if the applicant has omitted any former employers from the application form. This is a sure sign of problems.

When interviewing prospective bookkeepers, watch for their knowledge of accounting terminology. Many people claim to have bookkeeping experience when in reality they have simply handled accounts receivable, accounts payable, and payroll records. A full charge bookkeeper should be fully familiar with the terms "general ledger," "trial balance," "balance sheet" and the like.

A simple bookkeeping quiz will tell a great deal about the applicant's general knowledge. Exhibit 8-2 presents a bookeeeping quiz used by our firm for the past several years in testing applicants. A full charge bookkeeper should be able to complete this quiz with marks of nearly 100 percent.

Getting Help from Salesmen

Many times a client will need some type of a write-it-once system or even a bookkeeping machine. Salesmen who handle these products can be of great assistance to the accountant, but he needs to know how to deal with them. Salesmen know their products and can provide useful ideas in solving problems. Their primary function, of course, is to sell their products and their proposals must be evaluated with a critical eye.

It is desirable to call for proposals from more than one company in order to get ideas from two sources and the benefit of price competition. On the other hand, this requires additional time on the part of everyone concerned. Keep in mind, however, that the extra time spent is usually worthwhile and that the cost of installing a system or a machine must be considered an investment which will pay returns over future years.

The salesman's proposal must be evaluated carefully. Be sure he has spent sufficient time studying the present system and understands the client's objectives. The salesmen should have a clear understanding of such things as the number of transactions involved and the potential growth of the company. The accountant knows more about the client than does the salesman and should see that all facets of the problem have been considered.

A clear understanding should be reached with the salesman concerning installation. Let him know he is expected to spend sufficient time on the installation to see that it is functioning properly. Some salesmen are tempted to move on to the next job as soon as the sale has been made and neglect the proper follow-up on the installation. This is unusual, but it is well to make the point that the client expects a complete and thorough job in getting the system installed and functioning properly.

The proposal for a write-it-once system or a bookkeeping machine should include a design of all the forms to be used. The accountant should review these to see that there are complete accounting records and that the system is easy to follow. Some machine systems have been designed where figures cannot be traced. This is done for the sake of efficiency, but is false economy in the long run. Anyone who needs to review and examine the records will have to spend extra time at a cost exceeding the amount that was saved. Be sure the system is complete and provides all the accounting data necessary.

When to "Farm Out" Part of the Office Work

One of the solutions to an overloaded office is to consider having some of the work done outside. This normally involves sending it to a data processing service center. Some of the more common applications are discussed below.

Preparation of Payroll Checks—Any time the client's payroll exceeds about 25 people, the time and effort involved in preparation of checks and keeping payroll records become significant. One of the ways to solve this problem is to have a data processing center prepare the payroll checks. A by-product of this is the preparation of all payroll records. It is surprising how many employers are using manual systems and failing to take advantage of time-saving features that are available.

Accounts Receivable—There are many advantages to having accounts receivable prepared by data processing equipment. In addition to the preparation of customer statements various types of by-product information are available. Aged lists of accounts receivable can be easily prepared, as can analyses of sales by territory, by salesmen, by product line and the like. The computer can automatically add service charges to the account each month. Pharmacy accounts can show separation of medicines from other purchases, thus saving the druggist the headache of receiving many phone calls at the end of the year from customers wanting to know how much medicine they can deduct on their tax returns.

General Ledger Accounting—Chapter 6 discussed the rendering of bookkeeping service to the small client. If he wants to farm out this service, it should be done through his accountant. The accountant, of course, can handle it in his own office or can make use of a service center.

Inventory Controls—Perpetual inventory records can be maintained by a service center with the proper numbering system for the inventory items. The maintenance of perpetual inventory records is, of course, a detailed and time consuming job. It lends itself well to a service center operation. It does have to be handled very carefully, however, in order that the correct information is produced.

Farming out this type of work can produce a number of benefits. Frequently, the client can operate with a smaller office force as well as less office equipment and space. Farm out should especially be considered when the present office personnel are loaded with work and consideration is being given to the employment of extra personnel. The accountant should be alert and make appropriate suggestions to the client along this line.

Seven Specific Time-Saving Suggestions

Dropping Pennies—Some clients can use an accounting system where pennies are dropped; after all, business decisions are not made on pennies. It is generally necessary that the accounts dealing with the outside world be kept in pennies (accounts receivable, accounts payable, cash, payroll, etc.). On the other hand, income and expense accounts, fixed assets and certain other accounts can be kept in whole dollars. The pennies that have been dropped can be charged to a "penny difference" account. Significant time can be saved by not having to record or add pennies.

Checking Invoices—If the client is checking the figures on every supplier's invoice prior to payment, he may not be getting a good return on the time invested. It is generally satisfactory to check invoices only in the case of (1) large invoices and (2) invoices from new suppliers. The possibility of finding significant errors in other instances may be too small to make the checking worthwhile.

Check Signing—If two signatures are required, inquire as to whether both parties sign after the check has been prepared. If one party is signing blank checks, the procedure is of no value and should be discontinued.

Payroll—Consider changing weekly payroll to bi-weekly or monthly. The time saved in preparation of payroll checks and payroll can be very significant.

Elimination of Cash Disbursements Journal—Suggest that the client start using a three-part, voucher-type check. The third copy is filed by account number to be charged. The check copies are simply totaled monthly for cash disbursements purposes and the totals only are posted.

Accounts Payable—If the client pays his bills on time each month, discontinue the purchases journal and accounts payable ledger. When the bill is paid, charge the expense account directly at that time. If accounts payable figures are needed for the monthly financial statement, set them up by journal entry and reverse out next month.

Bank Reconciliations—Suggest the use of two bank accounts, each being used every other month. Reconcile each account only at the end of the "inactive" month, when there will be few if any outstanding checks. This especially saves time on accounts with a heavy volume of checks and is well suited to payroll accounts. Companies with a large volume of payroll checks each week can alternate accounts on a weekly basis.

Mr. Julius Lipsett
Quality Motor Co.
Brownsville, Texas

Dear Julius:

After having reviewed your office procedures with Mrs. Jones, I feel there are a number of things that can be done which would streamline the operation and save time. These suggestions are outlined as follows:

Cash Receipts - Discontinue entering detailed receipts in Cash Received Journal. Post only the daily totals from the Cash Book. Debit directly to Cash in Bank and discontinue entries transferring from Cash on Hand to Cash in Bank.

TIME SAVED - 1 TO 2 HOURS PER MONTH

Enter all cash received into receipt book. Make up a daily summary on the back of the receipt. Discontinue use of Cash Book and post summary directly to Cash Received Journal.

TIME SAVED - 1 TO 2 HOURS PER MONTH

Accounts Receivable - Your present system takes about eight hours per month for preparation of statements. By using either a small posting machine, a multi-posting board or a copying machine system you could prepare statements at the same time the customer's ledger is posted. The posting operation during the month would take a little more time, but there would be no time preparing statements at the end of the month.

TIME SAVED - 6 HOURS PER MONTH

In addition, you would be able to get statements in the mail sooner.

Further, it is recommended that the words "All accounts due and payable by 10th of the month following date of purchase" be printed on the statements, instead of using a rubber stamp.

TIME SAVED - 1/2 HOUR PER MONTH

Payroll - A separate series of check numbers should be used for payroll checks. Payroll checks, which are entered in detail in the Payroll Journal, can then be summarized in the Cash Disbursements Journal only once a month. At present, payroll checks have to be summarized in the Cash Disbursement Journal every time a payroll is paid, in order to keep the check number series intact.

Exhibit 8-1—Report on View of Client's Office

TIME SAVED - 1/2 HOUR PER MONTH

The use of a multi-posting board for payroll preparation is suggested, especially if such a board can be used for accounts receivable also. Use of such a board would make it possible to post the Employees' Earnings Record at the same time the payroll check is prepared.

TIME SAVED - 1 HOUR PER MONTH

The type of checks used with the multi-posting board would provide for a stub that the employee could detach showing the amount of his earnings.

If it is decided not to get a multi-posting board, we suggest obtaining a separate set of payroll checks with a stub the employee can detach. This would also enable use of a separate series of check numbers, as mentioned above.

Cash Disbursements - The Cash Disbursements Journal can be entered without writing in the name of the payee. This information is on the check stub and can be obtained from that source when needed.

TIME SAVED - 2 TO 3 HOURS PER MONTH

Parts and Service Sales - The practice of transferring totals each day from the Daily Sales Summary to the Parts and Service Sales Journal could be discontinued. These totals could be transferred only once a month.

TIME SAVED - 1 HOUR PER MONTH

Preparation of Financial Statement - The monthly financial statement requires numerous percentages and statistics. All dividing must be done by hand and all multiplication done by a rather slow method on the adding machine. If the adding machine were traded in on a printing calculator which would add, subtract, multiply and divide, these computations would go much faster.

TIME SAVED - 2 TO 3 HOURS PER MONTH

The amount of time that can be saved is an estimate, of course, but I believe it is realistic and fairly conservative. If you were to make all the changes outlined above, there would be a potential saving of 15 to 18 hours per month. Some of these suggestions require an expenditure of money and you will have to weigh the amount of money required against the amount of time that would be saved.

Also, some of these procedures will require some time to get set up and operating. In other words, in some cases it would take two or three months before the full benefit is obtained. Some of the suggestions, on the other hand, simply do away with duplicate posting of certain information. These suggestions should be adopted right away and the benefits should come immediately.

I will be happy to discuss these ideas with you further at any time.

Very truly yours,

Exhibit 8-1—Report on View of Client's Office (continued)

NAME_____

Date_____

LONG, CHILTON, PAYTE & HARDIN
BOOKKEEPING QUIZ
(FOR FULL-CHARGE BOOKKEEPERS)

1. Circle the one correct answer for each of the following questions.

   a. The total of all of the open balances on customers' accounts at the end of a month should equal...

Accts. Pay Acct. in Gen. Ledger	Accts. Rec. Acct. in Gen. Ledger	Sales Acct. in General Ledger	Purchases Acct. in Gen. Ledger	Purchases plus Sales

   b. When are Social Security tax returns filed?

      Weekly   Monthly   Quarterly   Semi-annually   Annually

   c. Calculate the interest at 6% on $750 for 60 days.

      $7.50 $11.25 $22.50 $45.00

   d. What is the maximum annual wage subject to unemployment tax in Texas?

      $3,000.00 $3,600.000 $4,000.00 $4,200.00 $4,800.00

   e. If the total of the outstanding checks at the end of a month is $50, the balance per the bank statement is $500, what is the book balance?

      $400.00 $450.00 $500.00 $550.00 $600.00

2. Circle "DEBIT" or "CREDIT" to indicate whether the following accounts would ordinarily appear as a debit or credit balance in the general ledger.

PURCHASES	Debit Credit	MERCHANDISE SALES	Debit Credit
ACCOUNTS RECEIVABLE	Debit Credit	CAPITAL ACCOUNT	Debit Credit
SALARIES	Debit Credit	DEPRECIATION EXPENSE	Debit Credit
PREPAID INSURANCE	Debit Credit	BONDS PAYABLE	Debit Credit
ACCRUED INTEREST PAYABLE	Debit Credit	NOTES RECEIVABLE	Debit Credit
LAND AND BUILDINGS	Debit Credit	FEDERAL WITHHOLDING	
DEPRECIATION RESERVE	Debit Credit	TAX PAYABLE	Debit Credit
CASH DISCOUNT ON SALES	Debit Credit	INTEREST EARNED	Debit Credit
ACCOUNTS PAYABLE	Debit Credit		

3. On the back of this page prepare general journal entries for the following transactions:

   a. Sale of merchandise on account for $200.00.

   b. Payment by check of salary; gross salary of $150.00, less withholding of $8.77 Social Security Tax and $20.00 Income Tax.

   c. Purchase of merchandise on open account for $150.00.

   d. Purchase of furniture and fixtures for $300.00, paid by check.

   e. Collection of $200.00 for merchandise sold in 3(a) above.

   f. Payment by check for merchandise purchased in 3(c) above.

Exhibit 8-2—Bookkeeping Quiz (for Full-Charge Bookkeepers)

CHAPTER 9

Preparation of Small Client Income Tax Returns

Reasons for Preparation of Small Returns

At the outset, it is suggested that the accountant consider his responsibility in regard to preparation of small returns. In order for our tax system to work, it is necesary for taxpayers to have access to competent professional help when necessary. The licensed or certified public accountant has an obligation to serve the public (he holds his license to practice because of the public interest). It seems to follow, therefore, that preparation of small client returns is a professional obligation and in the public interest.

This is not to say, of course, that the public must be served at a financial sacrifice. The practitioner should, and indeed can, prepare small tax returns on a profitable basis. Later in this chapter, we will discuss methods for rendering a profitable service.

Recent years have seen a new industry of commercial tax return preparers spring up around the country. These commercial firms are preparing tax returns on a profitable basis and professional accountants should be able to do the same. Professional accountants may have to charge a higher fee than the commercial firms, but can demonstrate that the quality of the service is well worth the fee.

In our practice, we find that during the tax filing season we are dealing with a much broader group of clients than during the rest of the year. Preparation of individual income tax returns provides an opportunity to serve the general public, which is not the case with auditing, accounting and corporate income tax work. There is considerable satisfaction in assisting a wide spectrum of individuals with their income tax problems.

The exposure to the general public enhances the accountant's reputation and image in the community. He becomes more widely known and generates additional sources of referrals. These referrals will frequently be additional income tax clients, but not always. There are occasions when an individual income tax client will be in a position to refer a job of substantial size to his accountant. Always keep in mind that a large part of the accountant's new clients come to him because of referrals by satisfied clients.

Special Problems in Preparation of Small Returns

The most significant problem encountered in preparation of individual income tax returns is that of getting the information from the client; getting all the necessary information, getting correct information, and getting it in a form that permits preparation of the return without excessive time. The accountant can educate his clients as to how to assemble the necessary material. There are points to be considered and problems to be overcome in this connection.

One problem concerns the client who brings in information that is incomplete. The preparation of the return must be held up while awaiting the missing data. This interferes with a smooth flow of work.

Another problem concerns the client who remembers certain additional information after the return has been completed. This is even more disruptive to the work flow and certainly requires an additional charge for the redoing of the return.

Another factor that greatly influences the fee is the quality of the material submitted by the client. Clients submit information in a tremendous variety of forms. Some bring in all their bank statements, canceled checks, paid bills, etc. They feel better if the accountant has looked over all of their material. Many others, of course, simply prepare a list of income and deductions from which the accountant can prepare the return quite readily.

Many of these problems can be overcome by a patient process of education. This is approached in different ways by different firms. In our firm, after the client has made an appointment, he receives a letter outlining some things he can do to cut down the time and cost involved in the preparation of his return. This letter (Exhibit 9-1) has proven to be very helpful in persuading our clients to get the information to us in better shape.

The firm of Lyda, Boyd, Starr and Wilson of Austin, Texas, uses a different approach. They send their clients several pages of material with the suggestion that the client prepare and insert the necessary information prior to his appointment (see Exhibit 9-2). This firm reports that many of their clients appreciate this opportunity to get their material ready.

Fee for Preparation of Small Returns

The subject of obtaining an adequate fee from the small client was discussed in Chapter 2. The general principles outlined in that chapter are, of course, applicable to all types of accounting service, including tax service. There are, however, certain special points that should be kept in mind regarding fees for preparation of small returns.

Some accountants use higher billing rates for income tax work than they do for auditing and accounting work. They feel that income tax work is of more direct financial benefit to the client and should bear a higher fee. Further, there is a great demand for service during a short period of time. The practitioner is required to staff his organization to take care of this peak work load as well as work long hours under hectic conditions. All of this justifies a higher fee than might be charged for other work under different circumstances.

If higher fees are to be charged for tax work, the practitioner will have to decide whether to use a special billing rate or whether simply to over-bill his normal rate. A special rate complicates the accountant's procedures for recording time. On the other hand, it might produce more revenue by insuring that the proper fee is billed. There are many firms using special rates, and many that do not.

Another point to keep in mind when billing individual returns is the amount of incidental service required by the client during the year. When you bill income tax clients, don't forget that many of them call you during the year regarding tax questions. Further, Internal Revenue Service computers now generate an endless stream of notices to taxpayers and many clients want their accountant to review any communication received from the Internal Revenue Service. The fee you charge for preparation of the return should make an allowance for these extra services.

How to Handle Tax Season Work Load

Tax season offers real challenges and opportunities and presents real problems. The work load increases substantially, which brings opportunities for increased profits. The organization of the office to handle the increased work in an efficient manner is of the utmost importance.

Perhaps the ideal way to handle an influx of small tax clients is to have a "small returns department." This would be a group of people given exclusive responsibility for handling this work. They could do a first-class job because they would be concentrating solely on individual returns. The personnel would become thoroughly familiar with the problems and procedures required.

Setting up such a department, however, is easier said than done. In most firms, the accounting staff is busy year-round with audit and accounting work and cannot be reassigned exclusively to small tax returns. It might be feasible, however, to assign one accountant to this function. One person working exclusively with small returns could accomplish a great deal. If the volume of work requires more than one person, try using part-time people working under the supervision of the full-time accountant. There are several different sources of part-time personnel. If there is a college in the community, junior- and senior-level accounting majors could serve quite well. Office workers in other industries are sometimes interested in part-time work. Retired people are sometimes available, as are housewives who are interested in temporary or part-time employement. Whether or not the accountant uses a "small returns department," the use of part-time personnel should be considered.

Overtime work during tax season is universal among accounting firms. There is a wide range, however, as to the hours worked, which seem to run anywhere from 45 to 65 hours per week. There seems to be a trend, however, to cut down on excessively long hours. Many firms are concluding that there is a loss in effectiveness when an accountant works more than 50 to 55 hours per week. We have worked about 50 hours per week in our firm for the past several years. It is clearly understood by everyone that these are the hours we will work, and somehow the work is accomplished during that period of time. In more recent years, we have worked a ten-hour day for five days per week and close the office on both Saturday and Sunday. The two days off during the weekend are appreciated by all concerned.

Techniques for More Effective Use of Time

The practitioner is subject to interruptions and hectic working conditions during tax season which can materially reduce his effectiveness and productivity. It is important to arrange the work day so that there are certain periods free of interruption. The accountant can't do justice to complex problems or meet deadlines without some time for concentration.

It is desirable to schedule appointments during certain specified hours insofar as possible. This leaves the other hours of the day for direct productive effort.

Telephone calls are a prime interrupting factor. It is wise to set aside certain hours of the day when telephone calls will not be taken. The calls can be returned later, and probably the secretary can handle some of them.

You have to remember, of course, the importance of being available to clients and staff. You can't cloister yourself behind closed doors for extended periods without causing some problems. You do, however, need some limited time during the day that is reasonably free of interruption so you can concentrate on important work.

Computer-Prepared Returns

A strong development in recent years in handling the tax-season work load has been use of computer-prepared returns. Many practitioners have gone this route and have found numerous advantages. Computerized returns are neat and accurate. They save the practitioner's time by relieving him of detailed computations. Also, the computer is programmed to check on certain elections, such as income averaging and the like.

On the other hand, there are certain disadvantages. One, of course, is the cost factor. Ideally, the practitioner will have saved enough time to cover the cost of the computer service. In actual practice, however, this is not always the case and the accountant must either take a write-down or the fee must be increased.

Some practitioners object to the procedures for submitting information to the computer bureau. The preparation of forms is in some respects nearly as complex as the preparation of the return itself. The accountant must do a sizable number of returns by this method in order to become familiar with the computer forms. In fact, if an accountant is going to computer-prepared returns, it seems best to go all the way and put everything on the computer.

Some accountants prefer to do returns manually because of less review after completion of the work. In the case of computer-prepared returns, it is necessary to review the return after it comes back from the bureau, which may be a week or ten days later. This step is not necessary with manually-prepared returns.

It seems clear, however, that more and more accountants will use computer-prepared returns in the future. Undoubtedly, the cost will decrease and the quality and scheduling of the service will improve. Some firms are preparing returns on their own in-house computers and this method also has increasing possibilities for the future.

Office Procedures for Small Tax Returns

The most important factor affecting a smooth flow of returns is the interview itself. It is imperative that the interviewer obtain complete information in order to eliminate telephone calls and additional visits with the client. It is easier to obtain complete information if the firm has educated the clients as to what is expected, as discussed earlier in this chapter. The interviewer must do a complete job, however, and should use an interview checklist to remind him of questions that could otherwise be overlooked.

The checklist used by our firm is found in Exhibit 9-3. It serves as an interview checklist as well as a record of certain information concerning preparations, processing and delivery of the return. We prefer a one-page checklist because it is easier to get our personnel to complete it properly. While it is not as extensive as checklists used by some firms, it serves our purpose. We revise it and run it on different colored paper each year. It is stapled to the front of our copy of the return and the different colored sheets make it easier to locate prior year's returns.

When a client has called in for an appointment, the secretary types in headings (name, address, etc.) on the current year's checklist form and on all forms used on the client's return for the prior year. All this material is in the file at the time of the interview.

Our returns are prepared in pencil on Internal Revenue Service forms and are then photocopied. Checking is, of course, done prior to copying so that errors can be corrected simply by erasing the pencil information on the forms. We have found that the use of electronic calculators in preparing and checking tax returns is much faster than the use of conventional adding machines.

The appearance of returns is better if headings are typed rather than printed. The typing can be done by a secretary, thus saving time of the accounting staff. Headings and descriptions can also be typed for depreciation schedules and any other lengthy material.

Conclusion

The small client most frequently needs the accountant's service because of tax problems. The preparation of income tax returns in a professional manner is the very heart of tax work. The accountant must become familiar with the problems in preparation of returns, know how to cope with the tax-season workload, adopt office procedures that provide for efficient operation and know how to charge a proper fee for this service. There is nothing more important in small client service.

LONG, CHILTON & COMPANY
Certified Public Accountants

MEMORANDUM

To: Individual Income Tax Clients

From: Long, Chilton & Company
       Certified Public Accountants

You will soon be coming to us for the preparation of your income tax return and this is written to provide information which we hope will be helpful in getting all the necessary information.

A considerable part of the cost of preparing your return is related to getting full, complete and correct information. There are a number of things you can do to help in this area.

First, it reduces our work if we can get all of your material at one time. Frequently, clients bring us material which is only partially complete for one reason or another. When this happens it necessitates additional visits or phone calls and delays the preparation of the return. This generally requires us to spend more time than would have been the case otherwise, thus increasing the cost to you.

Some of you have been bringing us bank statements, cancelled checks and paid bills. It is not necessary that we review this material unless you especially want us to. You can go through your checks, bills, deposit slips and other material, listing those items which need to be reported on your tax return. This will cut down on the time required by us. Some people even request us to make phone calls to get certain information, such as interest. This definitely increases the cost of preparing the return.

We recognize that you may not be familiar with how certain transactions are reported on your return. In fact, we often find that people fail to bring in certain information because they did not know it should be reported. If you have questions, call us ahead of time.

One very important point; don't come in until you are sure you have all the necessary facts. We have a surprising number of instances each year where we have completed someone's return and they later find some information they forgot to give us. This requires that the return be done again at an increased cost.

We want to prepare your return as economically and efficiently as possible. At the same time we want to reduce the number of problems we encounter during the tax filing season. This memorandum is sent to you, therefore, in the hope that it will enable us to work together more effectively to accomplish these ends.

Exhibit 9-1—Letter to Individual Income Tax Clients

INCOME TAX INFORMATION WORKSHEET FOR 19X3

Please submit data requested either in the space provided or in an attached memo.

	Name	Date of Birth	Social Security Number
Taxpayer	_____	_____	_____
Spouse	_____	_____	_____

Home Address _____

    (Number and Street) (City, Town, or Post Office) (County) (State) (ZIP Code)

Address to which return is to be mailed
   (If other than above)_____

Telephone Numbers: _____   _____
                    Business   Home

DEPENDENTS

   FIRST NAMES OF DEPENDENT CHILDREN WHO LIVED WITH YOU

   _____   _____

   _____   _____

OTHER DEPENDENTS

Name	Relation-ship	Months Lived in Your Home	Did Dependent Have Income of $750 or More	Will Dependent File A Return of His Own	Amount of Support Furnished By You	Amount of Support Furnished By Others Including Dependent
_____	_____	_____	_____	_____	_____	_____
_____	_____	_____	_____	_____	_____	_____

Occupation of Husband_____

Occupation of Wife _____

Did you, at any time during 19X3 have any interest in, or signature or other authority over, a bank, securities, or other financial account in a foreign country? /__/ Yes   /__/ No

/__/ Check here if you want a set of 19X3 blank income tax information worksheets mailed to you with your 19X3 return. Otherwise you will be mailed 19X4 worksheets early in January, 19X5.

/__/ Check here if taxpayer elects to contribute $1.00 of taxes to the next Presidential Election Campaign Fund.

/__/ Check here if taxpayer's spouse elects to contribute $1.00 of taxes to the next Presidential Election Campaign Fund.

Exhibit 9-2–Income Tax Information Worksheet

PAYMENTS ON 19X3 ESTIMATED TAX

_____Date_____	_____Amount_____
_____	_____
_____	_____

We usually base estimated tax on the prior year's tax in order to avoid any penalty for underestimation. However, if you expect your income next year to be materially different from this year's income, please let us know, and we will take the changes into consideration in preparing your estimate. Also, please let us know if you expect your exemptions to change because of an increase or decrease in dependents. If you have income tax withheld from your salary, we will assume that the withholding will be the same in 19X4 as in 19X3 unless we are otherwise notified.

WAGES:

Attach W-2's from Employer

If you received salary while you were absent from work on account of personal injury or sickness for more than 30 days, please furnish the following information:

Period of absence from work - From_____to_____
Were you hospitalized as a bed patient for at least one day during this period?_____
Regular weekly rate of pay _____
Number of workdays in your normal workweek _____
Name of employer_____
Amount received for period of absence on account of sickness _____

SOCIAL SECURITY RECEIVED

	Net Amount Received	Medicare Premiums Deducted	Gross Amount Of Soc. Sec.
Husband	_____	_____	_____
Wife	_____	_____	_____

ITEMIZED DEDUCTIONS - MEDICAL AND DENTAL EXPENSES

Premiums paid for insurance providing medical care

_____To Whom Paid_____	_____Amount_____
_____	_____
_____	_____
_____	_____
Medicare and medicaid premiums	_____
Medicines and drugs	_____

Exhibit 9-2—Income Tax Information Worksheet (continued)

We suggest that you list below only the amounts that you actually paid to physicians, etc., **without regard** to any insurance benefits paid directly to them and list as medical insurance **reimbursements** received only the amounts the insurance companies paid directly to you.

Please list payments to or for physicians, dentists, nurses, and other professional health **practicioners**, hospitals, transportation necessary to get medical care, eyeglasses, artificial teeth, medical or surgical appliances, braces, and X-ray examinations or treatment.

To Whom Paid	Amount
_____	_____
_____	_____

Medical insurance reimbursements received (list)

_____	_____
_____	_____

ITEMIZED DEDUCTIONS - TAXES   (Do not include in this section taxes in connection with a business, rent property, or a farm or ranch).

Real estate
   City taxes on home . . . .   _____
   School district taxes on home . . . .   _____
   State and county on home . . . .   _____
   Water district on home . . . .   _____
   Other real estate taxes in connection with investment
      property (list) (exclude business, farm, and rental
      property)

_____	_____
_____	_____

State gasoline tax (you may enter the number of miles
   driven) for personal purposes . . . .   _____

General sales tax except on automobiles purchased. (We
   will use table furnished by Internal Revenue Service
   unless you have kept up with a higher amount). . . . .   _____

Sales tax on personal automobiles purchased . . . .   _____

Personal property
   City and school district taxes on personal autos . . .   _____
   School district taxes on personal autos . . . .   _____
   State and county taxes on personal autos . . . .   _____

Federal excise taxes on personal expenditures, Federal social security taxes on domestic help, **hunting licenses**, auto inspection fees, auto licenses, driver's licenses, and taxes on alcoholic **beverages, cigarettes** and tobacco are not deductible.

Exhibit 9-2—Income Tax Information Worksheet (continued)

ITEMIZED DEDUCTIONS - CHARITABLE CONTRIBUTIONS

You may deduct gifts to churches, including assessments paid; Salvation Army; Red Cross; United Fund; non-profit schools and hospitals; Boy Scouts, Girl Scouts, other similar organizations. You may also deduct unreimbursed out-of-pocket expenses directly attributable to services you render to a charitable organization. Additionally, you may deduct 6¢ a mile for driving done for a charitable organization. You may also deduct up to $50.00 ($100.00 on a joint return) for contributions to political organizations or candidates. Property contributions are not eligible for the political contribution deduction.

You may not deduct as contributions gifts to relatives, friends, or other individuals; foreign organizations; social clubs; labor unions; chambers of commerce; or propaganda organizations.

CASH: Name   Amount

_____   _____

_____   _____

_____   _____

NON-CASH:

Name	Amount	Description Of Property	Date of Gift	Method of Valuation

For each non-cash gift of property valued at more than $200.00, certain information must accompany the return. Please attach a sheet setting out the following information:

        Any conditions attached to the gift
        Manner of acquisition of property
        Cost of other basis if owned by you for less than 5 years
        Signed copy of appraisal, if any

Indicate by placing * beside any amount listed for which you do not have a receipt or cancelled check.

ITEMIZED DEDUCTIONS - INTEREST EXPENSE (Do not include in this section interest in connection with a business, rent property, or a farm or ranch).

Home mortgage . . . .   _____

Other: To Whom Paid   Amount

_____   _____

_____   _____

Bank service charges are not deductible as interest.

"Points" for obtaining a new home loan are deductible when paid.

Exhibit 9-2—Income Tax Information Worksheet (continued)

ITEMIZED DEDUCTIONS - MISCELLANEOUS

Preparation of income tax return . . . .   _____

Safe deposit box rental . . . .   _____

Expenses in connection with production or collection
   of income (List).

        _____   _____

        _____   _____

Union dues . . . .   _____

Dues to professional organizations in connection with
   occupation (List).

        _____   _____

        _____   _____

Other (List)

        _____   _____

        _____   _____

Examples of other miscellaneous deductions are alimony, business publications, small tools used in employment, employment agency fees, and uniform costs including cleaning of uniforms.

A deduction for each personal casualty loss is allowed to the extent that the loss exceeds $100.00. The following information must be furnished in connection with casualty losses exceeding $100.00.

Type of casualty_____
_____

Type of property_____
_____

   Fair market value of property just before casualty   _____

   Fair market value of property immediately after
      the casualty . . . .   _____

Cost of property . . . .   _____

Insurance recoveries . . . .   _____

DIVIDENDS (Attach schedule if needed)

You may attach your Forms 1099 to this page instead of listing the dividends.

Exhibit 9-2—Income Tax Information Worksheet (continued)

CASH: Name of Company   Amount*
            _____   _____
            _____   _____
            _____   _____

MUTUAL FUNDS

                                                Non-
        Company   Total   Taxable   Capital Gain   Ordinary
    _____   _____   _____   _____   _____
    _____   _____   _____   _____   _____
    _____   _____   _____   _____   _____

Foreign income tax withheld from dividends . . . . _____

Tax withheld by regulated investment companies . . . . . . _____

*Indicate if you believe any of these dividends are wholly or partially non-taxable
 distributions. Please attach any pertinent correspondence or advices.

INTEREST INCOME:

You may attach your Forms 1099 to this page instead of listing the interest.

                Payor   Amount
    _____   _____
    _____   _____
    _____   _____

SALES OR EXCHANGES OF PROPERTY (Other than amounts listed on other schedules)

                        Date   Date   Sales
    Description   Acquired   Acquired   Date Sold   Price   Cost
_____   _____   _____   _____   _____   _____
_____   _____   _____   _____   _____   _____

If a security which you held became worthless during the year, list it above and put "Worthless" in the Sales Price column. The security must be entirely worthless. A deduction for
partial worthlessness of securities is not allowed. Indicate if the company was operating
under the Small Business Investment Act of 1958.

Also list any non-business debts which became entirely worthless within the taxable year.

If real estate was sold, we need copies of closing statements covering the purchase and sale.
Permanent improvements made to the property since acquisition should be added to cost of
property.

Principal collections this year on sales reported on the installment method in prior years:

Exhibit 9-2—Income Tax Information Worksheet (continued)

Property	Principal Collected This Year	Principal Balance At End of Year

List collections on each sale separately.

If you sold your residence during the year at a <u>gain</u> and <u>have purchased</u> or <u>will purchase</u> another residence, please supply the following information in additional to that called for at the top of this page:

Date you occupied or expect to occupy new residence   _____
Cost or expected cost of new residence   _____
Expenses in connection with sale of old residence   _____
Date construction began if you constructed new residence   _____

Expenses of selling old residence:

	To Whom Paid	Date Paid	Amount
Sales commission			
Advertising expense			
Attorney and legal fees			

Fixing-up expenses incurred for work performed within 90 days before the contract to sell was signed and paid not later than 30 days after the sale, solely to assist in the sale of the residence.

Description	Date Work Performed	Date Paid	Amount

PROFIT OR LOSS FROM BUSINESS OR PROFESSION

<u>If you have a double-entry set of records which you are furnishing to us, you may disregard this schedule except for the questions.</u>

Business Name_____

Business Address_____

Employer Identification Number_____

Are any business expenses claimed in connection with:

(1) Entertainment facility (boat, resort, ranch, etc.)?   /_/ Yes   /_/ No

Exhibit 9-2—Income Tax Information Worksheet (continued)

    (2)   Living accomodations (except employees on business)?   ☐ Yes   ☐ No

    (3)   Employees' families at conventions or meetings?   ☐ Yes   ☐ No

    (4)   Employee or family vacations not reported on W-2?   ☐ Yes   ☐ No

Gross receipts . . . .   _____

Returns and allowances . . . .   _____

Inventory at beginning of year . . . .   _____

Merchandise purchased . . . .   _____

Cost of merchandise withdrawn for personal use . . . .   _____

Labor . . . .   _____

Materials and supplies . . . .   _____

Other costs (list)

    _____   _____

    _____   _____

Inventory at end of year . . . .   _____

Expenses

   Taxes
      Payroll . . . .   _____
      Property . . . .   _____
      Sales tax on equipment purchased . . . .   _____
      Licenses . . . .   _____
      Other

      _____   _____

      _____   _____

   Rent . . . .   _____

   Repairs . . . .   _____

   Salaries . . . .   _____

   Insurance . . . .   _____

   Legal and professional fees . . . .   _____

   Commissions . . . .   _____

   Interest . . . .   _____

Bad debts (include only amounts previously
   reported on income).   _____

Exhibit 9-2—Income Tax Information Worksheet (continued)

PROFIT OR LOSS FROM BUSINESS OR PROFESSION (Continuation)

Expenses (Continuation)

Advertising . . . . _____

Dues and subscriptions . . . . _____

Janitor and cleaning . . . . _____

Laundry . . . . _____

Office supplies . . . . _____

Other supplies . . . . _____

Promotion . . . . _____

Telephone and telegraph . . . . _____

Travel . . . . _____

Utilities . . . . _____

Automobile (indicate whether amounts listed are <u>totals</u> or
    <u>business portions</u>)

Gasoline, oil, and servicing . . . . _____
Insurance . . . . _____
Repairs . . . . _____
License . . . . _____
Total miles driven this year . . . . _____
Personal miles driven this year . . . . _____
Business miles driven this year . . . . _____

EQUIPMENT, FURNITURE, AND FIXTURES ADDED THIS YEAR

Investment Credit

The Internal Revenue Code provides for investment credits upon acquisition of certain
depreciable personal property used in trade or business. Please list depreciable property acquired in 19xx.

Description (Indicate (N) new (U) used)	Date Acquired	Cost	Estimated Useful Life

EQUIPMENT, FURNITURE, AND FIXTURES SOLD THIS YEAR

Description	Date Acquired	Date Sold	Sales Price	Cost

Exhibit 9-2—Income Tax Information Worksheet (continued)

List details of any other business furniture and equipment trades or other dispositions during the year.

_____

_____

If you have a self-employed retirement plan, we will need Forms 4848 and 4849 filled out by the Trustee or information called for by these forms.

PENSIONS AND ANNUITY INCOME (Do not include social security)

NAME OF PAYOR	AMOUNT RECEIVED THIS YEAR
_____	_____

Information needed as to annuities received for the <u>first time this year</u>:

1. Your cost, if any _____
2. Amount per year which you will receive_____
3. Length of time you will receive pension or annuity_____
4. From whom received_____

INCOME FROM PARTNERSHIPS

Due to the complexity of the information required in reporting partnership income, it will be necessary for us to have copies of all returns (Form 1065) in which you own a partnership with years ending in, or with, 19X3.

EXPENSES which you paid in connection with partnerships and for which you <u>were not reimbursed</u>.

Automobile* (indicate whether amounts listed are <u>totals</u> or <u>business portions</u>).
    Gas, oil, servicing . . . . _____
    Insurance . . . . _____
    Repairs . . . . _____
    License . . . . _____
    Taxes . . . . _____
    Tires . . . . _____

Dues . . . . _____

Travel . . . . _____

Promotion . . . . _____

Other (list)

_____   _____

_____   _____

*Total miles driven during the year . . . . _____

Business miles driven during the year . . . . _____

Personal miles driven during the year . . . . _____

Exhibit 9-2—Income Tax Information Worksheet (continued)

If new car was purchased during the year, please furnish us a copy of the invoice.

INCOME FROM SMALL BUSINESS CORPORATION

Due to the variety and complexity of the information required in reporting income from interest in Small Business Corporations, it will be necessary for us to have copies of returns (Form 1120S) for all such corporations in which you own with years ending in, or with, 19X3.

INCOME FROM ESTATES OR TRUSTS   (If you can furnish us a copy of Schedule K-1 of Form 1041, you may disregard the information requested below as to your share of estate or trust income.

Name_____

Employer Identification Number_____

Dividends qualifying for exclusion . . . .   _____

Short-term capital gain . . . .   _____

Long-term capital gain . . . .   _____

Other taxable income (itemized)

_____   _____

Depreciation and depletion . . . .   _____

Foreign tax credit . . . .   _____

Other deductions and credits (itemized)

_____   _____

EMPLOYEE BUSINESS EXPENSES - TRAVEL AND TRANSPORTATION

Airplane, boat, railroad, etc., fares . . . .   _____

Meals and lodging . . . .   _____

Tips . . . .   _____

Taxi . . . .   _____

Parking fees and tolls . . . .   _____

Automobile expenses* (indicate whether amounts listed are
   totals or business portions)
   Gasoline, oil, lubrication, etc. . . . .   _____
   Repairs . . . .   _____
   Tires, supplies, etc. . . . .   _____
   Insurance . . . .   _____
   Interest . . . .   _____
   Taxes . . . .   _____

Exhibit 9-2—Income Tax Information Worksheet (continued)

Other (list)

_____   _____

_____   _____

*Total miles driven during the year . . . .   _____

Business miles driven during the year . . . .   _____

If a new car was purchased during the year, please furnish us a copy of the invoice.

Amount of reimbursement received   _____

OUTSIDE SALESMAN'S EXPENSES

Automobile* (indicate whether amounts listed are
   totals or business portions)

   Gasoline, oil, lubrication, etc. . . . .   _____
   Repairs . . . .   _____
   Tires, supplies, etc. . . . .   _____
   Interest . . . .   _____
   Taxes . . . .   _____
   Insurance . . . .   _____

Advertising . . . .   _____

Supplies . . . .   _____

Telephone . . . .   _____

Dues . . . .   _____

Conventions . . . .   _____

Gifts for customers . . . .   _____

Meals for customers . . . .   _____

Airplane, boat, railroad, etc., fares . . . .   _____

Meals and lodging while away from home overnight . . . .   _____

Tips . . . .   _____

Taxi . . . .   _____

Other (list)

_____   _____

_____   _____

*Total miles driven during the year . . . .   _____

Business miles driven during the year . . . .   _____

Exhibit 9-2—Income Tax Information Worksheet (continued)

If a new car was purchased during the year, please furnish us a copy of the invoice.

Amount of reimbursement received   _____

EDUCATIONAL EXPENSES

Education expenses are generally deductible if the education which is undertaken
(1) maintains or improves a skill required by the individual in his employment or other
trade or business, or (2) meets the express requirements of the individual's employer, or
the requirements of law or Regulations, imposed as a condition to the retention by the
individual of an established employment relationship status, or rate of compensation. This
is true even for education which leads to a degree.

However, expenses for education which are personal or capital expenditures, or have elements
of both are not deductible even though they may maintain or improve or may meet the express
requirements of the taxpayer's employer. Non-deductible capital or personal education
expenses are thos which: (1) are required of the taxpayer in order to meet the <u>minimum</u>
educational requirements for qualification in his present employment, trade, or business;
or (2) qualify the taxpayer for a new trade or business.

1. Name of education institution or activity _____
_____.

2. Address _____

3. Were you required to undertake this education to meet the minimum educational requirements to qualify in your employment, trade, or business?

         ☐ Yes   ☐ No

4. Will the program of study undertaken qualify you for a new trade or business?

         ☐ Yes   ☐ No

5. State the reason for obtaining the additional education and show the relationship
between the courses taken and your employment during the period _____
_____
_____

6. List the principal subjects studied at the educational institution or describe your
educational activity_____
_____

    Expenses (list)

         _____   _____

         _____   _____

MOVING EXPENSES

What is the distance from your former residence to your new business location? _____miles

What is the distance from your former residence to your former business location?
_____miles

Transportation expenses to move household and personal property   _____

Exhibit 9-2–Income Tax Information Worksheet (continued)

Travel, meals, and lodging expenses to move from old residence to new area of principal employment   _____

Pre-move travel, meals, and lodging expenses to search for a new residence   _____

Temporary living expenses in new location (or area) prior to moving into permanent quarters   _____

Expenses incident to: (Check one)

    (a) ☐ Sale or exchange of taxpayer's former residence; or

    (b) ☐ If nonowner, settlement of an unexpired lease on former residence   _____

Expenses incident to: (Check one)

    (a) ☐ Purchase of a new residence; or

    (b) ☐ If renting, acquiring a new lease   _____

Reimbursements and allowances received for this move (other than amounts included on Form W-2)   _____

RENTS: (Use one column for each property)

Kind and location of property			
Rent received			
Real estate taxes paid			
Insurance			
Interest			
Utilities			
Advertising			
Supplies			
Yard mtc.			
Repairs			
Painting			
Electrical			
Plumbing			
Carpentry			
Other			
Other expenses (list)			

Exhibit 9-2–Income Tax Information Worksheet (continued)

Additions to property and furniture and equipment (Do not include items listed above)

Description*	Date Acquired	Cost	Estimated Life

If real estate has been acquired during the year, we will need the following information:

Total purchase price (copy of closing statement will be helpful). . . . _____

Allocation of purchase price among
Land . . . . _____
Building . . . . _____
Furniture and equipment (insurance policies and city tax
   notices will be helpful) . . . . _____
Type of construction . . . . _____
Approximate age of construction . . . . _____
General condition of property when acquired . . . . _____

* Indicate (N) new (U) used

ROYALTY INCOME

Type of royalty . . . . _____

Gross royalty . . . . _____
Taxes
   Property . . . . _____
   Production . . . . _____
Other expenses (List)

_____   _____
_____   _____

FARM INCOME

Business name_____ Employer Identification Number_____

Location of farms and number of acres in each farm _____
_____

Farm income
   Sales of livestock or other items purchased for resale (not brood stock) which were sold*

Description	Quantity	Sales Price	Cost

*List and indicate cost of livestock purchased for resale which died during the year and show "Died" in sales price column.

Exhibit 9-2—Income Tax Information Worksheet (continued)

Sales of raised livestock and produce and other farm income

	Quantity	Amount
Cattle	_____	_____
Calves	_____	_____
Sheep	_____	_____
Swine	_____	_____
Poultry	_____	_____
Dairy products	_____	_____
Eggs	_____	_____
Wool	_____	_____
Cotton	_____	_____
Vegetables	_____	_____
Grain	_____	_____
Fruite and nuts	_____	_____
Mohair	_____	_____
Goats	_____	_____
Machine work	_____	_____
Patronage dividends	_____	_____
Agricultural program payments		
Cash	_____	_____
Materials and services	_____	_____
Commodity credit loans	_____	_____
Federal gasoline tax credit	_____	_____
State gasoline tax refund	_____	_____
Other		
_____	_____	_____
_____	_____	_____

Sale of purchased and raised brood stock*

Description	Date of Purchase or Date of Birth	Date of Sale	Sales Price	Cost
_____	_____	_____	_____	_____

*Also list purchased brood stock which died during the year and show "Died" in sales price column.

Expenses*

	Amount
Labor (Do not include labor on construction of permanent improvements)	_____
Repairs, maintenance (Do not include construction of permanent improvements)	_____
Interest	_____
Rent of farm pasture	_____
Feed purchased	_____
Seed and plants purchased	_____
Fertilizers and lime	_____
Machine hire	_____
Supplies purchased	_____

Exhibit 9-2—Income Tax Information Worksheet (continued)

FARM INCOME (Continuation)

Breeding fees . . . . _____
Veterinary and machine . . . . _____
Gasoline, fuel, and oil . . . . _____
Storage . . . . _____
Taxes . . . . _____
Insurance . . . . _____
Utilities . . . . _____
Freight and trucking . . . . _____
Soil and water conservation . . . . _____
Telephone . . . . _____
Dues . . . . _____
Other (List)

_____   _____

_____   _____

*Indicate personal portion, if any, beside each item and show only the business portion in the amount column.

Brood stock, machinery, equipment, and permanent improvements added during the year

Investment Credit:

The Revenue Act of 1971 provided for a credit of up to 7% against the Federal income tax for qualified investment in certain depreciable personal property used in a trade or business. Please list personal property acquired in 19X3.

Description (Indicate (N) new (U) used)	Date Acquired	Cost	Estimated Useful Life

*Include amounts paid to others to construct permanent improvements.

List details of any farm property or equipment trades during the year.

_____

_____

Number of gallons of gasoline purchased for nonhighway use   _____

Number of gallons of lubricating oil purchased for nonhighway use   _____

ITEMIZED DEDUCTIONS - CHILD AND DEPENDENT CARE EXPENSE

Child and dependent care expenses are "employment-related expenses" paid for the following expenses, but only if such expenses are incurred to enable you to be gainfully employed on a substantially full-time basis: (1) Expenses for household services, and (2) expenses for the care of a qualifying individual.

Exhibit 9-2—Income Tax Information Worksheet (continued)

Monthly expenses incurred for services <u>in</u> the household for one or more of the following dependents:

	Children Under 15 Years of Age	Disabled Dependent 15 Years of Age or Over	Disabled Wife (Husband)
January			
February			
March			
April			
May			
June			
July			
August			
September			
October			
November			
December			

Monthly amounts incurred for services <u>outside</u> the household for care of a child(ren) under 15 years of age. Number of children _____

January	_____	July	_____
February	_____	August	_____
March	_____	September	_____
April	_____	October	_____
May	_____	November	_____
June	_____	December	_____

Total amount of adjusted gross income and disability income received this year by your disabled dependent 15 years of age or over _____.

Total amount of disability payments received by your disabled wife (husband) _____

Were any of the expenses listed above paid to a related individual? ☐ Yes ☐ No
    If yes, please list the relationship and the amounts paid

_____   _____

OTHER INCOME (List)

_____Description_____   _____Amount_____

_____   _____

OTHER DEDUCTIONS (List)

_____   _____

_____   _____

Enter any income or deductions which appear not to fit on any other page.

Exhibit 9-2—Income Tax Information Worksheet (continued)

<u>TAX RETURN CHECK LIST</u>

FILE NO._____CLIENT PHONE NO._____DATE RECEIVED_____TAX FORM_____

NAME_____SS# H_____W_____

ADDRESS_____._____COUNTY_____

OCCUPATION H_____W_____YEAR OF BIRTH H_____W_____

NAMES OF DEPENDENT CHILDREN WHO LIVED WITH YOU_____

HOW MANY DEPENDENTS (1) LIVED WITH YOU?_____ (2) FILED A TAX RETURN?_____

PREPARE ON FASTAX_____ REGULAR _____ LIVE IN CITY LIMITS? YES_____NO_____

EXEMPTIONS - FILING STATUS

Joint _____
Single _____
Head of Household _____
Surviving Spouse _____
Separate returns _____

DEPENDENTS OTHER THAN MINOR CHILDREN

How many? _____
Name _____
Relationship _____
Residence _____
Income _____
Your support _____
Other support _____

(list on back if more than one)

INCOME FROM

Alimony _____
Annuities _____
Business (get I.D.no.) _____
Dividends _____
Estate or trust _____
  (get I.D. number) _____
Expense allowance and reimbursements _____
Farming (get I.D. no.) _____
Interest _____
Partnership (get I.D.no.) _____
Pensions _____
Rents _____
Royalties _____
Sales or exchange of property _____
Social security _____
Sub chapter "S" _____
Stock options _____
Salary _____
Other _____ _____

DEDUCTIONS FOR

Standard deduction _____
Contributions - cash _____
    - property _____
Medical - hospital ins. _____
    - medicine _____
    - doctors, etc. _____
    - travel _____
Taxes - real estate _____
    - sales tax _____
    - extra sales tax _____
    - gasoline _____
Interest _____
Casualty or theft _____
Child care _____
Education _____
Employee business expense _____
Investment expense _____
Moving expense _____
Retirement income credit _____
HRIO plan _____
Sick pay _____
Tools used on job _____
Union or other dues _____
Uniform _____
Bad debts _____
Worthless stock _____
Tax return preparation _____
Mileage - business _____
    - charitable _____
Political contributions
$1.00/2.00 to political party _____
Other _____ _____

Yes	No	
		1. Estimate filed for current year? Amount paid $_____.
		2. Amount of estimate for next year_____. If not filed give reason_____
		3. Form 2210 or 2220 attached?
		4. Foreign bank accounts?
		5. Did we prepare last years return?
		6. IRS exam? Years_____
		7. Investment credit for 19X3?
		8. Investment credit recapture?
		9. Carryovers from prior years?
		(a) net operating loss
		(b) capital loss
		(c) excess contributions
		(d) investment credit
		10. Tax preference items?
		11. Alternative tax on capital gains?
		12. Maximum tax on earned income?
		13. Income averaging?

SPECIAL INSTRUCTIONS:_____
_____
_____
_____
_____

Due date of return_____   Client name to be charged_____

Date promised_____

Number of copies_____

Send bill for_____

Bill later_____

Delivery instructions_____

Date mailed, delivered or picked up
_____By_____

Called or notified to pick up_____
          (Date)

	Initials	Hrs.	Date	Amt.Billed
Prior time				
Interviewed				
Prepared				
Prepared Reviewed				
Checked				
Reworked				
Rechecked				
Fastax charge				
TOTAL				

CHECK IF ADDITIONAL MATERIAL WRITTEN ON BACK_____

FOR CORPORATIONS: Answer questions 1 through 11

FOR INDIVIDUALS: Answer questions 1 through 13

Exhibit 9-3—Tax Return Checklist

CHAPTER 10

Assisting the Client with Tax Planning and Tax Problems

The tax field provides varied opportunities for rendering significant services to small clients. Tax planning can be of real benefit in several areas; planning for the proper type of business organization, setting up qualified retirement plans, advance planning on major transactions such as sale of property or sale of a business, and estate planning. Assisting the client with tax examinations is an especially important service. This chapter discusses techniques to be used in performing these services and, where necessary, convincing the client of the need for them.

Need for Tax Planning

Any experienced practitioner can relate stories of clients who entered into major transactions without tax planning or tax advice. The tax problems created by such action are often serious and sometimes disastrous. The accountant must educate his clients to discuss proposed transactions in advance. Many clients are strongly motivated and like to take action quickly (sometimes too quickly). After one or two expensive mistakes, of course, they become more tax conscious. The accountant's job, however, is to help the client avoid those expensive mistakes in the first place. This is where client education becomes important.

You should stress with clients at every opportunity the need to advise you in advance of any major transactions. This should be brought home time and time again. Every means of communication should be used, including the client newsletter. If you find a good article on the subject, you can make copies of it and mail to certain clients. The practitioner who makes a serious effort will find ways to keep his clients on their toes tax-wise.

Important Factors in Tax Planning

The areas of tax planning discussed in this chapter have one important point in common: it is imperative that you have all the facts. It is only too easy to give tax advice based upon incomplete or erroneous information. In any tax-planning situation, always ask plenty of questions, request copies of contracts and other documents and consult with attorneys to be sure that you have the complete and accurate story. Otherwise you could give a client bad advice.

Another important factor is the need to take a look at the long-range implications of your recommendation. For example, a client with a profitable business can frequently save taxes by incorporating. He should always be told, however, that five or ten years down the road his corporation may have built up all the retained earnings it could possibly use. At that point, the client is faced with the problem of how to get earnings out of the corporation at the least possible tax cost. Be sure that you have thoroughly explored not only the immediate tax-saving opportunities, but have looked at the client's situation several years down the road. If there are tax problems facing him in the future, he has the right to be fully informed about them.

Be careful about giving off-hand advice regarding complex tax questions. Some clients attempt to get "instant" advice (either because they hope to keep the fee down or they think the accountant can answer any questions immediately). It is frequently tempting to venture some off-hand ideas or suggestions. This is dangerous, however, because the client may act upon this off-hand advice, even though you may have cautioned him about the need for further study. If the client acts on the advice and it turns out to be wrong, he is going to blame the accountant regardless of the circumstances. It is better to advise the client that the matter needs further study and research, and to let him know how long it will take.

Estate Planning

One of the neglected fields of tax planning is estate planning. It is natural for clients to ignore this rather distasteful subject. Also, there is a lack of expertise in the subject on the part of many accountants. Both of these problems can be overcome by appropriate action.

It is not easy to discuss the subject of estate planning with a client. It must be done with tact and finesse. He should be advised that estate planning is not simply a matter of saving taxes. The subject in its broadest sense involves a determination of the client's assets and how they can best be transmitted at death. Estate planning considers the payment of taxes and elimination of excessive administration expenses, as well as determination that property will pass to beneficiaries as harmoniously and conveniently as possible. There are also lifetime benefits to be derived from estate planning. These include increased funds for retirement and a feeling of satisfaction in having one's affairs in order.

Estate planning is not just for millionaires. With the increase in values of property in recent years many people will be surprised to find their estates in the taxable range. There are a large number of small and moderate estates, which increases the opportunities for this type of service. Keep in mind also that the small owner has as many, if not more, reasons for planning than the wealthy one. In a small estate, taxes and administrative costs must be kept as low as possible so the survivors will have adequate funds. The accountant should, therefore, acquaint his smaller clients with the advantages that are available through estate planning. Our firm has regularly mentioned estate planning in client bulletins and this has made some clients more conscious of this need. One of the articles appearing in a client bulletin is found in Exhibit 10-1.

A written communication will serve as a reminder to the client but, generally, will not motivate him to take action. This usually has to be initiated by the accountant on a personal basis with the client. There are certain occasions when the subject can be appropriately brought up. One such occasion is the preparation of personal financial statements. It is here that the client's net worth is clearly outlined and is an ideal occasion for the accountant to make some comment regarding estate planning. The preparation of business financial statements and business or personal income tax returns can also be an occasion to raise the question. It is necessary to bring up this delicate subject in the right context so that the client is not offended by it. To do so, you have to be alert for the right occasion.

The use of a gift- and estate-planning questionnaire will serve as a reminder to the acccountant and his staff that this subject be considered for certain clients. The firm of Monroe, Shine & Company, New Albany, Indiana, uses a questionnaire found in Exhibit 10-2. This firms's procedures require that the questionnaire be prepared for each new client and reviewed annually with the old clients. The use of such a questionnaire for a selected group of clients would be of material advantage to any firm.

Estate planning is a field where the accountant, the lawyer, the bank trust officer and the life underwriter all play their parts and should work together as a team. The accountant is generally closest to the client, however, and sees him more regularly than do the others. The accountant is also familiar with the client's financial situation and income tax problems. He is able to coordinate both income tax and estate planning. In most cases, therefore, the accountant is the one who should take the initiative in discussing estate planning with the client.

The attorney must see that the will and other documents will carry out the client's objectives. The trust officer should be invited to assist in planning due to his familiarity with investment, financial and fiduciary matters. Where life insurance becomes a factor, its many uses should be thoroughly explored with a qualified life underwriter.

Estate planning requires above-average skills in understanding people and dealing with them. The client's personal desires, motivations and attitudes are extremely important. Always remember that the client is boss. For example, he may not want to make substantial gifts, even though such gifts would provide tax benefits. Remember, it's the client's property and he has the final say. Your responsibility is to make sure he understands the various tax benefits available to him.

Keep the estate plan as simple and practical as possible. It is easy to become over-enthusiastic and create a plan that is needlessly complex. No client should be put in a position of giving away property he will need for his own support in later years, or paying fees or other costs that are in excess of what they will save.

Tax Planning for Business Operations

One important aspect of tax planning for the business man is that of advising him as to the proper type of business organization. While tax planning is not the only consideration, it could be the most important. Certainly no client should choose a form of business organization without considering the income tax effect.

The situation most frequently encountered in this regard is whether or not to incorporate. This is a decision that is faced by all business and professional men who succeed in getting into high tax brackets. In giving advice on this subject, the accountant must become thoroughly familiar with all aspects of the situation. It is quite simple, of course, to make tax computations indicating the tax saving to be achieved by use of a corporation. It is necessary to probe deeper, however, in several areas. Here are some questions to ask:

> How much of the earnings of the business will be retained over a
> period of years as increased capital?
> How long does the present owner anticipate operating the com-
> pany?
> Does he have family members to whom he can turn over the
> business upon retirement?
> Will he sell to outsiders?
> What about selling an ownership interest to key employees?
> Is the owner interested in offering a good retirement plan to
> employees?
> How much hazard does the business present from the standpoint
> of legal liability?

All of these questions should be considered in deciding whether or not to incorporate. The client must be fully advised as to the tax benefits offered by incorporating, as well as told of any added taxes (such as state taxes) that will have to be paid. He should also be told of any problems to be encountered five or ten years down the road in case he wants to sell the corporation at that time. Further, he should be advised that operating as a corporation requires more self-discipline and care than is required of a sole proprietor. He should be advised of his status and responsibilities as an employee, officer and director of a corporation, and told of restrictions regarding withdrawal of corporate funds.

Careful planning is also required prior to entering into any major business transaction. Some examples are sale or purchase of corporate stock, sale or purchase of real estate or sale or purchase of a business. Generally transactions of this magnitude can be structured in alternative ways, some of which will provide significant tax benefits. It is important to educate clients to be conscious of the tax effect of such major transactions and consult with the accountant in advance.

The accountant can also render a valuable service by assisting in setting up a qualified pension or profit-sharing retirement plan. Small clients may not be aware of the tax advantages of such plans. There are a great variety of plans available and the accountant can advise the client as to the advantages and disadvantages of each. This is an area where many salesmen are hard at work selling their particular programs, and where the client could very well make the wrong choice.

Rendering advice in such areas as estate planning and qualified retirement plans requires specialized knowledge. It is important that someone in the accounting firm be designated as a specialist in these fields. This person should be given responsibility for becoming knowledgeable and keeping up to date. If the firm is not of sufficient size to justify such specialization, the accountant should then call in an outside specialist. In no event should advice be given by someone who is not thoroughly knowledgeable.

Handling of Income Tax Examinations

One of the most important services an accountant can perform is assisting the client with an income tax examination. In this situation, most clients feel on the defensive and are uncomfortable dealing with an Internal Revenue Agent. Many clients prefer that their accountant handle as much of the work in connection with the examination as possible.

One important ingredient in dealing successfully with Internal Revenue Agents is to have their respect before the examination begins. Your own reputation as a tax practitioner establishes the degree of respect you can command. If you are known as an accountant who strives to get all the information from the client and who prepares returns carefully, your effectiveness will be greatly increased. Agents are also impressed by the accountant who has an adequate tax library and a good command of tax law.

You cannot expect, of course, to settle all problems with Internal Revenue Agents based only on your reputation. There will always be honest differences of opinion in interpreting factual situations, tax laws and regulations. The Agent who respects your ability, however, is likely to raise only those issues which have merit and is not likely to harass the client or try to take advantage of him.

It is important during an examination to provide the Internal Revenue Agent with good records that can be easily reviewed. A good set of records and files in which paid bills and other material can be easily located speeds up the Agent's work. An agent who finds records and supporting data in good order will often complete the examination in a short period of time with less likelihood of raising questions.

On the other hand, an Agent confronted by poor records and lack of sufficient supporting data can easily become frustrated. This frustration may evidence itself in proposals for additional tax. It is only logical that an Agent who has to spend a great deal of time digging through poor records is more likely to present the client with a proposal for additional tax. We, therefore, advise our clients to make every effort to provide the Agent with the material he wants in the best possible order so that he can review it readily and complete his examination in the shortest possible time.

If you have audited the client, your audit file can be a useful tool during the examination. A good audit file contains information that is helpful to the Agent. He can quickly review the trial balance, adjusting entries and the verifications and analyses you have performed on the various accounts. A review of the audit file enables the Agent to complete his work promptly. This is, in fact, one reason for a client to have an audit.

In connection with providing information to the Internal Revenue Agent, always keep in mind that you have no requirement or responsibility to provide any information except that which he has requested. The Agent should be given the accounting records and supporting data he wants and should be given forthright answers to the questions which he asks. The accountant need not provide any more information than is requested and should not make comments that might lead the Agent into new areas. There is nothing underhanded or dishonest about this procedure. There are many areas in the tax law in which differences of opinion can arise and where the accountant will recommend a course of action that is favorable to his client. An Internal Revenue Agent might decide the same point in favor of the government, thus creating a point of dispute. Keep in mind, therefore, that your job is to give the Agent the information he requests but nothing more.

When the Agent requests information from your files, it is best to give him only the specific items he wants, not the entire file. Your file may contain memos or notes concerning research you have done on certain transactions, which would alert the Agent to a sensitive point. Generally the Agent will request only your file copies of returns or certain work papers, and this is all you should give him—not the entire file.

Some firms have their files organized so that copies of returns are in a "tax file" and other material is in a "correspondence file." This arrangement has the advantage of permitting the accountant to give the Agent the entire tax file, which contains nothing but copies of returns.

Your dealing with the Internal Revenue Agent should always be on professional terms. Even though you have an adversary relationship, it can still be one of friendliness and mutual respect. You should avoid any personal recriminations or heated disputes, which generally work to your disadvantage and your client's. Differences of opinion can be discussed on a professional level, concentrating on the issues at hand rather than on personalties.

What to Do When You Can't Agree with the Agent

Every effort should be made to reach agreement with the Internal Revenue Agent. This is not always possible, however, and the accountant must make a recommendation to the client about appealing the case to a higher level. The Internal Revenue Service has personnel whose function is to confer with taxpayers and their representatives regarding issues in dispute.

The primary factor to be considered in whether to appeal is the cost involved in relation to the potential benefits. The amount of tax due is a key factor. The client and the accountant must consider the amount of time that will be required to prepare for and attend the conference as well as the distance and travel expense involved. If these amounts seem reasonable in relation to the potential tax benefits, this would indicate a go-ahead. Another factor to be considered is the nature of the issues involved. Some issues can be negotiated and a compromise settlement reached. Other issues are clear black and white; either the taxpayer wins or loses, with no middle ground for negotiation and compromise. If, for example, there is only one issue which cannot be negotiated, it is necessary to evaluate the chances of winning. If the chances of winning are less than fifty-fifty, there is a serious question as to whether to go ahead with the appeal.

Careful preparation must be made for the conference—the accountant should carefully research the cases and rulings on all points in dispute. He must be well prepared regarding both the facts and the tax laws. The Conferee's job is to settle the case if possible and he is willing to give full consideration to a well prepared presentation. At the same time, he will not settle the case in your favor unless your argument and position are stronger than the Agent's.

If there are several issues involved or issues that can be negotiated and compromised, determine in advance the type of compromise you would be willing to accept. Be prepared to suggest a possible compromise settlement at the proper time. In this type of situation, it is almost always possible to reach a settlement that leaves the taxpayer in a better position than he was in before.

In presenting your case to the Conferee, do not be critical of the Agent. You may feel that the Agent's position is unjustified or disapprove of the manner in which he conducted the examination. These matters are not the responsibility of the Conferee, however, and there is little he can do about it. If anything, you are likely to prejudice your case by criticizing an Internal Revenue Service employee to one of his colleagues. This is not a professional way to handle a tax dispute and should be avoided.

Conclusion

Tax work is the backbone of small client service. Good service requires knowledgeable planning for income tax and estate tax matters, as well as ability to assist the client in tax examinations.

LONG, CHILTON & COMPANY

CLIENT BULLETIN

THE NEED FOR ESTATE PLANNING

An increasing number of people are recognizing the importance of a carefully
prepared estate plan. Such plans provide better security and benefits for
family members and hold inheritance taxes to the lowest possible level. Anyone should be in a position to answer the following questions:

How much am I worth at this time?

What would be the size of my estate considering life insurance proceeds?

How much will estate taxes and administration costs amount to?

Will there be enough cash available to meet all the needs?

Are the beneficiaries of my estate capable of handling it once it is
   in their hands?

Is my will up to date and does it actually do the job as intended?

Often after an estate plan has been prepared it is assumed that the job is
completed. Unfortunately, however, numberous changes occur over the years
that cause these plans to become obsolete. The plan should be reviewed,
therefore, from time to time.

Here are some of the changes that can make the plan obsolete.

Marriage of a child.

Death of a child.

Death of a spouse.

Ill health of child or spouse.

Significant increase or decrease in net worth.

Significant change in type of property owned.

Significant change in business relationship with partners or others.

Many people prefer to ignore estate planning. This can create problems
between family members as well as become very expensive. If you have not
faced to up this situation we urge you to do so.

Exhibit 10-1—Client Bulletin

MONROE SHINE & CO. - CERTIFIED PUBLIC ACCOUNTANTS
NEW ALBANY, INDIANA - BEDFORD, INDIANA   1.

GIFT AND ESTATE PLANNING QUESTIONNAIRE

This form should be prepared for new clients and also in cases where the client is interested in estate planning.

NAME_____

DATE_____

	YES	NO	N/A
1. Does the taxpayer understand that placing property in joint name with spouse with right of survivorship, except for real estate, cash and brokerage accounts may constitute a taxable gift?_____			
2. Does the taxpayer realize that if he has a federal estate tax problem, he should consider making gifts of life insurance policies he owns (including the assignment of group life insurance)?_____			
3. Should the taxpayer(s) consider a program of gifts of other assets in order to reduce the effect of federal estate and state inheritance taxes?_____			
4. Would a short term trust have any appeal to the client? (a gift of property in trust for a period of ten years by a high bracket tax-payer can keep the assets and income in the family and yet produce important savings in income and estate taxes.)_____			
5. Should the client consider a private annuity (an arrangement whereby property is transferred to another party in exchange for an un-secured promise to make periodic payments to the transferor)?_____			
6. If the taxpayer is affluent, should consideration be given to establishing a tax exempt family foundation? _____			
7. Did you consider after preparation of the estimated estate values on the next page whether the taxpayer is in need of general estate planning in order to pass his estate to his descendants at a minimum tax cost and in such a way as to accomplish his objectives?_____			
8. Should the client, if eligible, consider the adoption of a qualified deferred retirement plan? _____			
9. Should U. S. Treasury Bonds, available at a substantial discount, be acquired to pay Federal Estate taxes of the client?_____			
10. If the taxpayer has a closely held business interest, should he arrange his estate, if possible, so as to qualify under Sec. 303 and Sec. 6166? _____			
11. Should testator consider establishment of trust for closely held stock such as approved by U. S. Supreme Court in the Byrum case?_____			

Exhibit 10-2—Gift and Estate Planning Questionnaire

ESTIMATED ESTATE

DATE

ASSETS	TAX BASIS	(H)	FAIR MARKET VALUE (W)	(JT.)	TOTALS
Cash	$	$	$	$	$
Savings accounts					
Securities					
Personal effects					
Real estate					
Residence					
Life insurance					
Other assets (Describe)					
———					
———					
———					
———					
———					
TOTAL ASSETS	$	$	$	$	$

LIABILITIES					
Accounts payable	$	$	$	$	$
Notes payable					
Mortgage payable					
Other liabilities (Describe)					
———					
———					
———					
———					
TOTAL LIABILITIES					
NET WORTH					
TOTAL LIABILITIES AND NET WORTH	$	$	$	$	$

(NOTE) It is contemplated that the figures secured in a client interview for the purpose of completing the form above will be, for the most part, broad estimates, useful only for the purpose of determining whether a need for estate planning exists. If the rough estimates above indicate opportunities for planning in which the client is interested, a joint appointment with our office, the client and the client's attorney should be scheduled for the purpose of developing more precise information and proceeding with the formulation of a plan.

Exhibit 10-2–Gift and Estate Planning Questionnaire (continued)

CHAPTER 11

Small Client Financial Budgeting

We now begin to move into areas where the accountant can help the small client in management problems and profitability. Tax, auditing, and accounting are important services which must be performed well. The practitioner who wants to do a superior job, however, must also assist his clients in various areas of management services. Here is where the accountant ceases to be an overhead expense and becomes a profit-generator. This is clearly where the accountant becomes indispensable.

The services discussed in this and the succeeding chapters are sometimes referred to as "public controllership." The accountant becomes the client's financial advisor, helps him with his financial management. This is a natural by-product of other services provided by the accountant. The small client has no one in his organization with comparable ability, and frequently is not oriented himself toward financial management. Indeed, it may be his weakest point, one in which he desperately needs assistance. Many studies have shown that a large percentage of small business failures have occurred because of poor financial management.

One of the most valuable management services the accountant can render is assisting the small client with financial budgeting. This chapter describes the nature of the service and how to perform it for the small client.

What Is Budgeting?

The explanation of budgeting that can best be understood by the small client is that it is a system of planning and control. The accountant uses many terms to which the small client can't relate: balancing, reconciling, posting, confirming, etc. He probably associates these terms with his overhead expense: at best, he has trouble associating them with profits. The term "control" is something the client understands. He realizes he needs controls; he wants to control expenses and various other facets of his operation. When discussing budgeting, therefore, the accountant should stress the advantages of controls.

Planning and control is the game plan for modern management in large, successful companies. Budgeting is the heart of their system of planning and control. Large companies could not operate without sophisticated planning and control systems and are fully aware of their importance.

Budgeting consists of making the best estimate of all elements of income, costs and expenses, developing these into a profit objective plan for the year, and then comparing with actual results. This system enables management to make plans in advance rather than simply reacting to problems when they arise.

Financial budgeting is, in effect, planning for profits. A company does not usually make profits accidentally. The profits must be planned for and the most effective planning tool is the financial budget.

Fitting the Small Client into This Picture

It can be stated without question that any business is better off with a budget than without one. A large complex business needs an elaborate budget. A small business also needs a budget, but one which is simple and meets its needs. A simple budget can increase the profits for the small client. Such a budget can be devised without a major effort on the part of the accountant or at a major cost to the client.

The term "budget" may scare a client. If so, use another term. There is nothing wrong with the term "forecast" or "projection." If a client is more comfortable with one of these terms, by all means use it.

Many small clients think they know all about their businesses and can do the necessary planning and controlling by instinct. There may be some truth in this, but experience has proved that systematic planning and controlling will give better results every time. Indeed, it may be the key to survival. It is the heart of the financial management of the company, and can prevent fatal mistakes.

Small clients will be concerned about the cost of budgeting. The initial cost of setting up a budget is, of course, something to be considered. This is a one-time cost, however, and should be looked upon as an investment. After the budget has been prepared the first time, the client and his personnel can be instructed to do the bulk of the work in the future. In the long run, increased profits arising from good planning and control will far out-distance the cost involved.

The small client may feel he doesn't have a staff capable of dealing with the budget. Here again, a small company will have a simple budgeting system. It must be designed so that it can be handled by the client's personnel.

Another problem that may bother the small client is a feeling that the budget will restrict him. A budget is simply a plan of action; not something that must be adhered to in all circumstances. Situations will arise that were not anticipated when the budget was prepared; in such cases, the budget need not be followed. A knowledgeable manager learns to use the budget as a valuable tool without being limited in his flexibility. It should be understood that the budget may be deviated from when circumstances require it, but that it should be followed except when there is clear reason to deviate.

Budgeting Helps the Client Get Organized

The budgeting process requires the client to review his organization. Frequently, it will reveal situations where responsibility and authority guidelines are not clear, or where responsibility can be delegated to subordinates through the budgeting process, thereby relieving top management of certain operational details. Take the example of the client who operates two stores, each of which has a manager. The budgeting process will require consultation with each store manager to determine how much he feels his sales and costs will be. It follows logically that the store manager will be given responsibility for meeting certain sales objectives and holding certain expenses within budgeted amounts. Regular reports will compare actual results with the budget. As long as everything is in line, no other management action is required. This is the valuable management technique known as "management by exception."

The budgeting process, therefore, identifies areas of responsibility that might be overlooked otherwise. It provides an opportunity to delegate responsibility to key people and hold them accountable for reaching certain objectives. Thus, the client's organization is sharpened up and management becomes more effective.

How the Accountant Should Work with the Client

A successful budgeting program requires the accountant to deal very carefully with the client and his personnel. The psychological factors in a budgeting program are vital to its success. It is necessary that the budget have full support of the client—otherwise it will not succeed. Each person who is responsible for meeting certain goals and objectives must participate in the budgeting process. Budget preparation is not a one-man job for the accountant. It must be a joint effort with the client and his key personnel. A manager who is, for example, expected to hold his advertising expense to six thousand dollars will feel much better about this target if he has participated himself in determining it. If it is simply handed to him by the accountant or by the boss it will be resented. Therefore, two cardinal principles must be followed: (1) obtain the full support and participation of the top man in the organization and, (2) be sure that the top man and all key personnel participate in the budgeting process.

The first time a budget is prepared the accountant will, frequently, be heavily involved. This should be done with a view to reducing such participation in the future. The accountant may very well be involved in the budgeting process on a continuing basis, but it is best to do so in a limited way after the first installation. There are two reasons for this: (1) the cost to the client will be minimized if his own people can do more of the work; (2) the accountant is an outsider and it is best to hold outside participation to a minimum and let client personnel determine their own budget objectives.

On the other hand, the accountant should not install a budgeting system and then simply walk away from it. He needs to stay in contact with the client to see that the system is being properly followed. After the budget has been installed, reports must be prepared regularly to compare the objectives with the actual performance. The accountant should see that these are being prepared promptly and that a new budgeting process is instituted at the proper time. The client and his people may tend to become preoccupied with other things and not follow through with the budget for the following year if the accountant does not stay behind them.

Another important role of the accountant is to see that the budget is based upon realistic targets. If goals are based on undue optimism, the net effect may be more harm than good. Some clients are born optimists and are tempted to prepare their budgets based on what they hope will happen. Such optimism must be tempered by a realistic appraisal of the situation. It may very well be the accountant's responsibility to direct the client's thinking toward more reasonable expectations.

Cash Forecasting—An important by-product of the budget is the cash forecast. If the client is going to get into financial difficulties it will result in problems with cash. Here is the tool for controlling cash, for keeping the ambitious client from over-extending himself. Or if the forecast indicates an excess of cash, there is time to plan in advance for its utilization or investment. A cash forecast is extremely valuable in negotiating with lenders for both short-term and long-term borrowing.

Sometimes a client who is not using an operating budget will need a cash forecast (usually for borrowing purposes). The forecast in this context should be viewed as more limited in scope than an operating budget. The latter is a vehicle for planning and controlling operations, while the forecast is an effort to predict cash movement for a specified period of time.

The preparation of the forecast does, however, involve covering some of the same ground as preparation of the budget. The accountant must become familiar with the client's recent cash transactions. It is important to obtain knowledge of such areas as sales volume, inventory changes, accounts receivable collection history, and the like. If the forecast is prepared without this background information, the results could be inaccurate. A poorly done forecast is of no value and is probably worse than no forecast at all, since it is likely to mislead the client and others.

Accurate cash forecasting becomes more difficult as it projects further into the future. In case of a forecast for a twelve-month period, the last six months should be viewed with some skepticism because of unforeseen changes in conditions. The best procedure is to update the forecast every three to six months, taking recent developments into consideration.

The cash forecast gives the client a clear picture of his "cash flow." Cash flow is a popular term in the business world, indicating the cash generated from operations. One point should be made to the client, however; cash flow is not the same as profitability. It is possible to have a satisfactory cash flow on a temporary basis while incurring an operating loss and heading for trouble. The cash forecast should clearly indicate the differences between cash generated from operations, as opposed to cash funds borrowed or arising from sales of assets and the like.

A cash forecast is shown in Exhibit 11-1. Note the format arrangement showing cash generated from operations, as opposed to other sources. This illustration is in condensed form, and can be expanded as needed.

Budgeting for Non-Profit Organizations

Accountants usually become members of a number of organizations, some of which they serve as treasurers or as auditors. They can render a valuable service to these organizations by assisting them in their budgeting process. Surely, a well-prepared budget is extremely important to a non-profit organization, which does not have the profit element as a control factor. It is more difficult, therefore, to determine the proper level of expenses and how much income will be available.

One problem in preparing budgets for organizations such as churches is the tendency to budget for the program the organization would like to accomplish, and hope that sufficient money comes in to make it possible. While a proposed budget on such a basis is useful in trying to raise funds, it is not satisfactory for operating purposes. After the funds have been raised, the budget should be revised based on a realistic assessment of the income available. Expenses then can be set based on the resources and goals of the organization. This type of budgeting procedure will serve the organization best in the long run.

Many non-profit organizations have inadequate accounting and reporting systems and the accountant can provide a valuable service here. Up-to-date, informative reports are very important to the good administration of a non-profit organization. They help keep the board members and general membership informed of the financial status. It is always demoralizing to an organization to have reports which are not correct or do not give the information that is necessary for proper management. Exhibit 11-2 provides an example of a well-designed financial report of a church.

Use of Budgeting by the Accountant Himself

The accountant will generally have to sell the client on budgeting in order to get him interested in it. One question that the small client might reasonably ask the accountant is whether or not he uses budgeting in his own operation. If the practitioner does not feel that budgeting is of value for himself, the client could very well feel the same way.

In our firm we have used budgeting for many years and are sold on it. Some years ago the writer prepared an article which appeared in the "Practitioner's Forum" of *The Journal of Accountancy* on this subject, entitled "Budgeting for Profit in Accounting Firms." This material is quite pertinent for accountants interested in doing more budgeting work, and the article is as follows:

BUDGETING FOR PROFIT IN ACCOUNTING FIRMS

Budgeting has been called the most significant tool accounting provides to increase profits. Most CPA's would agree with this statement. They have prescribed budgeting programs for their clients, the client has used the prescription and it has worked.

It would be interesting to know how many CPA s are using their own medicine. How many are like the lawyer without a will, the doctor who won't go to bed when sick? How many CPA's are getting along with an inadequate set of books, infrequent financial statements, no budget?

In our firm we try to practice what we prescribe. We think it is good medicine and will help us. But there is another reason. If we make full use of accounting for management purposes, we can prescribe it for clients with more confidence. Furthermore, we have gained experience in working out our own problems that can be applied to clients' problems. If a CPA is going to be able to convince a client of the need for a budgeting program, he must first be fully convinced himself, preferably by experience with a successful application. What better place to begin than in his own office?

Budgeting is an integral part of planning and control of operations in our office. The budget is, of course, prepared at the beginning of each fiscal year. In working out the budget figures, many facets of the coming year's operations are considered. These might be overlooked or neglected without this planning program. For example:

Fees Billed—The big problem here is estimating the potential billing for the coming year. A look at prior year's records, current work in progress, the outlook for gaining new clients or losing present clients provides a basis for the estimate. A further help is in breaking the projection down in the following different ways:

1. By individuals in the firm.
2. By quarter of the year.
3. By type of service.

Making an estimate of billings by individuals in the firm gives a good idea of what can be achieved with the present staff. It must be tempered in light of those conditions that will reduce the maximum potential billing, such as idle time, unprofitable engagements, etc. This also provides a good occasion to measure performance of personnel in the firm, and to give people a goal to shoot for.

An estimate of billings by quarter is helpful in determining what periods of the year the billing will occur in and will facilitate comparison with actual billings through the year. The quarterly estimates can be based to a considerable extent on past performance. For example, if the first and second calendar quarters have each been producing 28 percent of the annual billing and the third and fourth have each been producing 22 percent, it is reasonable to assume that a similar pattern can be expected in the coming year. It is not too satisfactory to project billings on a monthly basis, since they fluctuate up and down with the completion of work.

An estimate of billings by type of service will be helpful in determining the areas of activity that may change. Some years, for example, bring more activity than others in tax cases and examinations. If the firm is trying to do more work in management services, an increase in billings might be expected in this area. If bookkeeping work is done, is it expanding or being reduced? All these points need consideration in working out the estimate of billings.

Once the billing projection has been prepared, it serves as a guide in setting up figures for many of the expenses.

Salaries—This, of course, is the largest single item of expense and must be considered carefully. Here are some points to be covered:

1. Will the present staff be adequate to produce the anticipated billings?
2. How much fee production can be expected from each person in the office?
3. Which staff members should receive salary increases? When should these increases come and in what amounts?
4. How much overtime will be required?
5. Should temporary or part time people be used instead of paying overtime?
6. How much should be budgeted for bonuses?

Library—This expense is reviewed to determine what is being spent currently, followed by an evaluation to determine whether the firm is getting its money's worth. It should also be determined whether the firm is too conservative in spending for library purposes, or is spending too much. Further, an evaluation should be made as to amounts spent for tax publications, as opposed to management, auditing and general books and periodicals. A reasonable balance should be maintained among these types of publications.

Dues—Does the firm belong to the necessary professional organizations? Should more participation in local organizations by budgeted? Are dues being paid that provide no benefit? A review is necessary each eyar to obtain the best value for the money spent.

Professional Meetings—This is an area that definitely needs to be planned in advance. Attendance at professional meetings should not be on a haphazard basis. Budgeting this item necessitates deciding how many people will attend CPA conventions, who will go to tax seminars, how many professional development courses will be participated in.

Office Supplies—The expense is rather sizable, and is frequently made up of numerous small, diverse purchases. It can be budgeted as a percentage of gross fees billed. Or the account can be analyzed to determine the cost of various categories of supplies. Certain questions can be raised for discussion, such as saving money by quantity purchasing, buying from mail-order suppliers, preparing internal forms on duplicating equipment, etc. It is easy to get into a rut in purchasing supplies, and the firm that is alert can find ways to save money.

Maintenance of Office Equipment—This item is reviewed to determine the best way of getting the maintenance job done. Are service contracts in effect? Are the charges reasonable? Is maintenance being deferred or slighted, with possible harmful effects on the equipment at a later date?

Insurance—The amounts and types of coverage are reviewed to determine need and adequacy. This is a matter of reviewing insurance in the same way it would be done for a client. If the firm maintains an insurance register, it will help in this review.

Telephone—Adequate telephone service is vital. Does the firm have a sufficient number of lines? Does everyone who needs an instrument have access to one? Are there any instruments that are not needed? Other points can be reviewed, such as telephone book listings, use of specialized telephone equipment, etc.

Occupancy—Space requirements need to be reviewed and cost of occupancy determined. Further, improvements to the office—either to increase attractiveness or efficiency—can be considered.

New Furniture and Equipment—An up-to-date accounting firm needs up-to-date equipment. The firm's present equipment can be reviewed with an eye to what needs to be replaced and new equipment to be added. This is a good time to work out a program for the year.

Initial work on the budget ordinarily would be handled by one partner.

While an elaborate group of schedules is not necessary, the various projections should be worked up in reasonable detail. This provides a basis for answering questions raised by other partners and can serve as a guide when the next year's budget is tackled.

The initial budget is then presented to the other partners for review. This review by all partners is the heart of the whole program. If the budget is given serious study by all concerned, is changed where necessary, and is finally agreed upon without serious reservations, it becomes a plan for the year. If, however, some partners are disinterested, its effectiveness as a management tool will be reduced.

Finally, regular comparisons of the budget with actual results must be provided. This can be done quite easily by comparing the budget with a monthly operating statement. Some of the budget schedules, such as payroll, will have to be set up on a monthly basis, and others will simply be allocated equally over the 12 months. The budget comparison for fees billed should be compared either monthly or quarterly, depending on how the budget was set up.

SOUTHWEST MERCHANDISING CORPORATION
CASH PROJECTION
January through June, 19X5

	January	February	March	April	May	June
Cash Generated From Operations						
Cash sales	$ 10,000	$ 11,000	$ 11,000	$ 11,000	$ 10,000	$ 12,000
Accounts receivable collections	18,000	18,500	18,500	18,000	19,000	19,000
Miscellaneous income	500	500	500	500	500	500
	$ 28,500	$ 30,000	$ 30,000	$ 29,500	$ 29,500	$ 31,500
Deduct:						
Merchandise purchased	$ 18,000	$ 20,000	$ 25,000	$ 24,000	$ 18,000	$ 19,000
Operating expenses	7,000	7,500	7,500	8,000	8,000	8,000
	$ 25,000	$ 27,500	$ 32,500	$ 32,000	$ 26,000	$ 27,000
CASH FLOW FROM OPERATIONS	$ 3,500	$ 2,500	$(2,500)	$(2,500)	$ 3,500	$ 4,500
Capital Transactions						
Sales of assets	$ -0-	$ 100	$ -0-	$ -0-	$ -0-	$ 0-
Financing of equipment purchases	-0-	-0-	-0-	-0-	-0-	0-
	$ -0-	$ 100	$ -0-	$ -0-	$ -0-	$ -0-
Deduct:						
Note payments	$ 800	$ 1,000	$ 1,000	$ 1,000	$ 1,000	$ 1,000
Purchases of new equipment	600	1,200	-0-	-0-	-0-	1,000
	$ 1,400	$ 2,200	$ 1,000	$ 1,000	$ 1,000	$ 2,000
DEFICIT FROM CAPITAL TRANSACTIONS	$(1,400)	$(2,100)	$(1,000)	$(1,000)	$(1,000)	$(2,000)
INCREASE (DECREASE) IN CASH	$ 2,100	$ 400	$(3,500)	$(3,500)	$ 2,500	$ 2,500
SHORT TERM BORROWINGS (REPAYMENTS)	(1,000)	-0-	-0-	5,000	(2,000)	(3,000)
NET INCREASE (DECREASE)	$ 1,100	$ 400	$(3,500)	$ 1,500	$ 500	$(500)
CASH - BEGINNING	8,000	9,100	9,500	6,000	7,500	8,000
CASH - ENDING	$ 9,100	$ 9,500	$ 6,000	$ 7,500	$ 8,000	$ 7,500

Exhibit 11-1—Cash Projection

CENTRAL UNITED CHURCH
BUDGET REPORT
Seven months ending July 31, 19X5

	JULY	YEAR TO DATE	BUDGET TO DATE (7 Months)	ANNUAL BUDGET
Receipts				
Budget offerings	$ 5,544	$ 43,913	$ 44,311	$ 75,792
Miscellaneous income	49	379	580	1,000
	$ 5,593	$ 44,292	$ 44,891	$ 76,792
Expenditures				
Worship Commission	$ -0-	$ 381	$ 758	$ 1,300
Outreach Commission	38	84	336	575
Evangelism Commission	16	295	761	1,305
Education Commission	113	1,217	1,502	2,575
Stewardship Commission	-0-	-0-	58	100
Finance Commission	74	686	1,152	1,975
Property & Maintenance Committee	772	4,779	5,347	9,166
Parsonage Committee	31	718	933	1,600
Pastors and Staff	3,537	22,453	22,244	38,138
Office Expense	36	1,137	817	1,400
Support of Other Causes	-0-	8,298	10,883	18,658
	$ 4,617	$ 40,048	$ 44,891	$ 76,792
EXCESS OF RECEIPTS OVER DISBURSEMENTS	$ 976	$ 4,244		

Exhibit 11-2—Budget Report for Church

CHAPTER **12**

A Financing Program
for the Small Business

The small client frequently needs to borrow money. Often he is not familiar with the various types of financing available or the type best suited for his situation. He may not be familiar with the requirements of lending institutions and may not present his loan request to the best advantage. He may arrange the wrong type of financing from the wrong source with poor repayment terms and high interest rates. Finally, he might be borrowing money unnecessarily.

This chapter deals with the specifics of helping the small client in his financing program.

Does the Client Really Need a Loan?

Some clients need loans because they are not properly utilizing their resources. Look at the assets on the balance sheet. Are there additional sources of funds that could be tapped? Inventories may be too high; accounts receivable could be staying on the books too long. Some clients tend to get overloaded with equipment. A program of strict inventory control, better collection effort and resisting the urge for new equipment could provide sufficient funds to make the proposed borrowing unnecessary.

In many instances, however, the need for a loan is valid and should be pursued. Surely, the accountant should never discourage borrowing money for a legitimate purpose. He can be the "devil's advocate," however, asking probing questions about the purpose of the loan.

Many loans are for some type of expansion. The accountant should ask questions about the proposal; its objectives, its potential and the cash requirements.

And most important of all, inquire about the client's plans for repayment. Don't let him think only about the great things he can do with the money; confront him with the problems of repayment. There should be a clear understanding of where the money is coming from for this purpose.

Determining the Type of Financing Needed

The financial world is dynamic and always changing. There are a great many types of financing available. The client should be advised as to different plans and which are best suited for him.

One approach that should be considered is whether to take in a partner or sell stock rather than borrowing money. There are definitely occasions when equity financing should be considered. This not only brings in permanent financing that does not have to be repaid, but may bring in a valued associate who can be of assistance in the management of the company. In some cases, the new investor may work full time, and in other instances he may be only an advisor.

Sale of stock to employees also has possibilities. While it may be difficult to raise significant sums by selling stock to employees, it is a means of tying them to the company and giving them more incentive.

In most instances, of course, the client will borrow money rather than sell stock. Questions then arise as to what type of financing is needed. Consider first whether to use long-term or short-term financing. Obviously, the choice is dictated in large measure by the reason for borrowing the money in the first place. If equipment is to be purchased or physical facilities constructed, the borrowing will normally be long-term. If working capital funds are necessary to finance a seasonal inventory or accounts receivable build up, short-term debt is the logical way to go.

The most important factor is to keep the client from getting tied up with repayment terms that he cannot reasonably expect to meet or from borrowing on unfavorable terms.

Determining Where to Apply for Financing

The client should borrow where he can get the amount of money he needs, a reasonable interest rate and repayment terms that fit his ability to pay. This is not always possible to arrange, but there is nothing wrong with shopping around for a loan. The lender has money for rent and wants to rent it out at the best deal for himself. The borrower wants to rent money on the best possible terms, just as he would in renting a building or a piece of equipment.

The cost of borrowed funds can be confusing. The "add on" rate used frequently in installment financing of automobiles and other equipment is expensive and should be avoided whenever possible. Some lenders charge for points, service or brokerage fees, various insurance premiums and the like. All these items increase the cost of borrowing. It is best whenever possible to pay simple interest on the unpaid balance, without any "extras."

The client should normally borrow money from the bank where he does business. He has funds on deposit and is already a customer. He should request the loan from his own bank in preference to going to a bank where he has no account. The second bank always questions why the applicant has not borrowed the money from his own bank.

Some clients will have bank accounts in different communities where they have branches or departments located. This should be looked upon as a secondary source of financing, especially financing that is related to the operation in that community. The writer has on occasion discussed financing problems with clients whose borrowing with their own local bank was up to the bank's limit. In some instances it has been suggested that the client apply to a bank in another community where he had a separate operation and maintained a bank account.

The client should consider financing programs made available by the federal government and other governmental bodies which are set up to encourage small business. The best known program, of course, is that of the Small Business Administration. Financing is also available from small business investment companies (SBICs) which are private corporations licensed by the Small Business Administration. The National Marine Fisheries Service has a program for financing companies in the fisheries of the United States in order to encourage this industry. There are also various local, state and regional development bodies which offer financing to businesses in order to strengthen them or attract them into a specific area. Information concerning these various programs can be obtained from the appropriate governmental body.

If the client wishes to borrow long term funds for the financing of buildings, equipment or long term working capital, he should consider life insurance companies, savings and loan associations, pension funds, various foundations, investment trusts or charitable organizations.

Sources of short-term financing of inventories and receivables are commercial finance companies or factors. It is possible to set up a revolving fund based on borrowing a percentage of outstanding accounts receivable or inventory in stock. The client is provided with a more or less permanent type of working capital financing which may be reduced or repaid whenever he is able to do so. Financing of this type is generally expensive but is very flexible.

Determining How Much to Borrow

One of the most difficult problems in connection with financing is knowing how much is needed. Borrowing too much money can prove to be expensive, especially where there is a penalty for early repayment. For some clients it is dangerous to borrow too much money because they will spend it whether they need to or not. On the other hand, borrowing too little money can get the client further into debt without solving his problems. When financing is needed it should be obtained in the proper amount—not too little and not too much.

The best method for determining what is needed is to prepare a cash projection. If the client has a budgeting program as discussed in Chapter 11, the preparation of the cash projection is a comparatively simply follow-up step. If there is no budget, the client's financial history and prospects must be explored in some depth in order to get the facts for the proper preparation of the projection. A cash projection is only as good as the research, study and thought that go into it. A carelessly prepared projection can be far off the mark and do more harm than good.

Preparation of Material to Submit to Lenders

Normally, the small client will look to his accountant for the preparation of the material to be submitted. Frequently, the client will request only financial statements because the bank has asked for them. The accountant can suggest additional items of useful information, however. Some of these are discussed below:

Historical Data—Even though financial statements should be prepared in comparative form reflecting the prior years figures, historical data over a period of five or more years is extremely useful. This will generally require a separate schedule such as that found in Exhibit 12-1. The accountant can determine the type of material that best suits the client's particular situation but many of the items presented in Exhibit 12-1 will be useful for the majority of clients.

Receivables and Payables—An aging of accounts receivable and accounts payable is extremely useful. If helps the client analyze his own situation, especially when compared with prior periods, and it helps the lender to understand the client's financial status and problems.

Inventories—The ratio of inventory turnover, as well as a breakdown of inventory by major items and an aging are quite helpful.

Comparison with Industry Statistics—It is always important to compare the client's company with others in the same line if reliable statistics are available. Such statistics can be obtained from various sources and the accountant must be familiar with these. Care must be used, however, to present comparisons that are meaningful. If the statistics are not good comparisons, their use might be misleading. An example of a presentation of meaningful comparisons with industry statistics is found in Exhibit 4-4.

Examination of Various Items on Financial Statement—If fixed assets are a significant portion of the total assets or are to be used as collateral, a schedule of them should be included. It is also desirable to give market or appraisal values as supplementary information. An example of a financial statement with supplementary appraisal information is found in Exhibit 12-2.

Significant liabilities and reserves, if any, should also be explained. All notes payable should have a full explanation of the interest rate, collateral, and due date.

History and Description of the Company—If the lender is not thoroughly familiar with the client's operation, a written history and description of the company will be very helpful. This should cover the date formed, a history of the company's growth, facts about the management, officers, products, markets, customers and competitive position.

Helping the Client in His Relations with the Lender

Normally, the accountant will be more experienced in dealing with lenders than the client. He can, therefore, help in establishing a satisfactory relationship with the lender and keeping it in good standing through the years.

Many points discussed in the preceding paragraphs are pointed directly to creating good relations with the lender. There are also certain human factors to consider and techniques that can be employed.

Most lending institutions and their officers deal with a large number of borrowers. They do not have the time to be thoroughly familiar with each borrower and his company; further, they do not always take the time and sometimes do not have the ability to analyze properly the financial information which has been presented to them. The burden is, therefore, on the borrower to take the initiative in seeing that the proper information not only is presented, but that it is adequately explained to, and is understood by, the lender.

The accountant can provide a valuable service by accompanying the client to meetings where a proposed loan is discussed. Frequently, the accountant can clear up points of confusion regarding the client's financial status or plans. A professional explanation of some unclear point in the financial statement can sometimes break a stalemate in loan negotiations. In such meetings, the accountant frequently has the best understanding of the client's financial situation and the most objective viewpoint on the proposed loan.

One problem about borrowing money is that the client almost always needs it immediately. There is time pressure on the accountant in preparing the information and on the lender in analyzing it and making a decision. This does not lend itself to good relations.

It is surprising how few clients make arrangements for a line of credit prior to the time they actually need it. It is good planning to arrange for financing well in advance, when both the client and the lender have adequate time to get acquainted, get information together and explore all the problems. The lender will surely be impressed with a borrower who has the foresight to arrange for money before he needs it.

The accountant can also help the client maintain a continuing relationship with the lender. Once a line has been established, the lender should be kept informed of developments. Interim financial statements should be provided, as well as information on new products or other significant changes in operations. All too often, everyone takes the line of credit for granted. Sometimes it will get out of line before an officer in the lending institution discovers what has happened. There is generally then a scramble to get the amount of credit back in line. This requires time-consuming negotiations and some change in the credit relationship, which often presents problems for the borrower. This type of problem can be avoided by keeping the lender continuously informed of what is going on.

Our firm has attempted to educate clients by discussing these matters in a client bulletin. This bulletin is found in Exhibit 12-3.

SOUTHWEST WHOLESALE, INC.
HISTORICAL DATA

	19X4	19X3	19X2	19X1	19X0
Working Capital	$ 234,110	$ 198,192	$ 179,397	$ 148,307	$ 122,425
Stockholders Equity	252,170	208,997	186,876	150,473	126,396
Net Profit	67,427	55,057	59,964	43,939	19,351
Return on Invested Capital	29 %	28 %	36 %	32 %	15 %
Inventory turnover	8.3 times	9.5 times	8 times	6.5 times	6.8 times
Sales volume	1,627,549	1,244,717	999,486	806,409	688,172
Accounts receivable Percent of Annual Sales	14 %	14 %	19 %	14 %	13 %

Exhibit 12-1—Historical Data

QUALITY DEVELOPMENT CORPORATION
STATEMENT OF FINANCIAL POSITION
June 30, 19X4

ASSETS	COST AND BOOK VALUES	CURRENT APPRAISAL VALUES
Cash on deposit	$ 81,694	$ 81,694
Due from stockholder	2,763	2,763
Work in progress - construction costs	126,406	131,750
Real Estate		
Plaza Street property	$ 38,615	$ 38,615
Wilson Road property	28,100	28,100
Gulf Boulevard property	215,617	642,000
Earnest money deposit	10,000	10,000
	$ 503,194	$ 934,922

LIABILITIES

Accounts payable, including estimated costs to complete houses	$ 92,282	$ 92,282
Accrued interest on notes	3,042	3,042
Notes payable	377,593	377,593
	$ 472,917	$ 472,917

STOCKHOLDERS' EQUITY

Capital stock - 5,804 shares at $10.00	$ 58,040	$ 58,040
Net loss for the year	(27,762)	(27,762)
Appraisal surplus	-0-	431,727
	$ 30,278	$ 462,005
	$ 503,195	$ 934,922

Exhibit 12-2—Statement of Financial Position

LONG, CHILTON, PAYTE & HARDIN
CLIENT BULLETIN

We have assisted clients on many occasions over the years in preparing financial
statements and other data to be submitted for credit purposes. As a result of
this experience, we have developed some ideas as to the type of information a
lender might need when considering a request for credit.

One point should always be borne in mind. The lender is probably not as familiar
with your company as you might think. He deals with many borrowers and cannot
take time to personally investigate all of them. It is to your advantage to keep
him well informed about your business. Here are some of the things that he may
need to know.

Nature of your company and its products - A concise written statement covering the
following points would be helpful and informative:

    (1) A brief history of your business and description of products and services
        offered.
    (2) The area of your market.
    (3) The number of persons you employ, the nature of their work and the labor
        turnover record of the company.
    (4) Growth possibilities.
    (5) Personal history of the officers or owners, including business experience.

Financial statements - Current financial statements are usually requested and usually
provided. A great deal of helpful information in addition to the regular statements
can be provided, however, such as:

    (1) Comparative figures showing changes in income, expenses, profits and
        financial position over a period of two to five years.
    (2) A statement showing changes in working capital over the past year, and
        the nature of the changes.
    (3) Various ratios, such as inventory turnover, percentage of profit earned
        on invested capital, etc.

It should be pointed out, also, that in the case of larger loans, or unsecured loans,
audited financial statements are encouraged. Audited statements carry more weight in
that the CPA accepts a higher degree of responsibility for the figures than the case
of non-audited statements.

Ability to repay - The main thing the lender is interested in is ability to repay.
Even though the loan may have collateral, the lender is not interested in repossession,
but in repayment. If your loan is to be repaid from earnings (as many loans are), it
would be most helpful if you could submit a projection of your income and expenses for
the period of repayment. You should provide an indication of the amount of earnings
available to repay a loan. This is especially valuable if yours is a seasonal business
and your loan is to be repaid from profits to be earned during your heavy season, or
from liquidation of a seasonal inventory.

Borrowing money requires planning, just like any other phase of business management.
Many loans are turned down because of lack of adequate information. A well prepared
loan application doesn't guarantee getting a loan, but it gets you off to a running
start.

Exhibit 12-3—Client Bulletin

CHAPTER 13

Providing Special Services to the Small Client

Nothing is more challenging and satisfying than spotting a problem for a client and helping him solve it. For the imaginative accountant here is an unlimited variety of opportunities. Here is the chance to contribute to the client's profits, thus making him enthusiastic about the value of your services. Performing special services successfully, however, is easier said than done. Success requires two important ingredients; organization and competence.

Organizing Yourself to Perform Special Services

One of the biggest problems in performing special services is simply the fact that the work is "special"—it is non-recurring. The practitioner who has audit and tax responsibility generally finds it difficult to put in the time and concentration necessary to complete a special assignment. Most local accounting firms do much less of this work than their clients need. One local firm that has set up a separate management services department (starting with one full-time staff man) has stated they did so because they became convinced the firm was not meeting the needs of their clients. The reasons the needs were not being met were as follows:

1. Audit and tax personnel were too busy with their own work and deadlines.
2. They lacked the competence required to perform management services work.
3. Personnel of the firm were not trained to recognize potential areas where the firm could be of service to clients.

It is essential for the practitioner to recognize the non-recurring nature of special services. The ideal arrangement for handling this problem, of course, is to have special personnel; a department or a staff man who devotes himself 100 percent to management services. This man should have no continuing client responsibilities; he should take on only special, non-recurring jobs for clients who are the continuing responsibility of other personnel in the firm. Once the special work has been completed, the management services man should move to other work.

For such an arrangement to be successful, the entire firm must be sold on it. Audit and tax personnel must be trained to be on the lookout for opportunities for special services. They are the sales people for this work. They must become conscious of client needs and be confident of the firm's ability to perform this work.

What does the practitioner do when he isn't in a position to utilize a full-time staff person for management services work? His best bet, probably, is to arrange his personal responsibilities to perform this work himself. Routine audit and tax work must be assigned to others, providing enough flexibility in the practitioner's own schedule to handle special work. This is not easy to accomplish along with other client and practice management responsibilities, and will become more difficult as the firm grows. At some point, separate personnel must be employed. An alternative in certain situations is for the firm to specialize in management services work, concentrating in serving clients in this area more heavily than in auditing.

Reaching an Understanding with the Client—It is probably more important to have a well-prepared engagement letter and a clear understanding with the client in special services than in any other type of work. Special assignments are unique; each has its own problems and objectives. The engagement letter should spell out the nature of the problem and the objectives to be attained. It is also desirable to define the assistance to be rendered by the client and his personnel.

The fee arrangement must also be clearly understood. Special services are generally done on an agreed per diem rate; it is difficult to predict the total fee in advance because of the non-recurring nature of the job. Estimate ranges are sometimes given, but the fee is generally based on a per diem arrangement.

Selling Special Services to the Client—As mentioned earlier, the other people in the firm should become the salesmen for special services. They are in contact with clients and aware of their needs. Most special engagements will probably be uncovered through the efforts of other staff members.

Personnel of the firm should show that their knowledge is sufficiently broad to get the job done. Some accountants give the impression of having a narrow view of the client's problems; one that is limited to accounting and tax matters. The accountant should expand his horizons and become known as a person with a wide range of knowledge and experience; one who is able to see beyond the books and tax returns.

Clients may not be aware of the range of services you can perform. Take steps to see that they become informed. This can be done in meetings where problem areas are pointed out and possible solutions are outlined. It is also done in a general way in the client newsletter. Our newsletter, for example, tells about the various courses our people attend. We feel this gives clients ideas about our abilities in various fields. Whenever a member of the firm speaks or writes on a particular subject, this is also mentioned in the newsletter.

When providing clients with this type of information, do so in a professional manner. Avoid the appearance of promotion or advertising. Don't over-sell the value of your services. Making grand promises that cannot be attained is a serious mistake. It is best to speak with confidence and realism concerning what you can do and what the client can expect from it.

The wise practitioner will try to create opportunities which make it natural for a client to seek advice. Reviewing a financial statement together, encouraging the client to get in touch any time, taking the client out for lunch, or dropping in to see him are natural ways to use this approach. It is also important to stress that the relationship with the client is confidential and that the client's information goes no further. This encourages the client to use the accountant as a sounding board for ideas.

Along the same line, rendering a continuing service to clients, rather than seeing him only at distant intervals, helps to create opportunities for special services. Stay in contact with clients as regularly as possible.

Steps in Performing the Engagement—A special services engagement stands a better chance of success if it is carried out by following established guidelines and careful procedures. This insures a well-thought-out and carefully performed job that delivers what the client wants. Here is a suggested list of steps to be used in an engagement from start to finish:

1. Initial review with the client in order to identify the problem.
2. Proposal letter to the client outlining the work to be done and the fee arrangement.
3. Field work.
4. Development of all alternate solutions.
5. Development of recommendations.
6. Implementation of recommendations.
7. Post-implementation follow-up.

The accountant should stress to the client the necessity of seeing the job through to the end. It is unwise to make recommendations and then disappear. Standard procedure for an engagement should be assisting with the implementation of recommendations to see that they are properly carried out.

SPECIFIC SUGGESTIONS FOR SPECIAL SERVICES WORK

As mentioned earlier, the opportunities for special services are limitless. A full discussion of all types of potential engagements is beyond the scope of this chapter. At the same time, brief discussions of several ideas are presented in order to stimulate the reader to look for needs among his own clients.

Helping the Client with Long-Range Planning

You undoubtedly have clients who are on "dead center," making no progress and not knowing what to do about it. This may be due to conservatism, being in a rut or being frustrated as to what steps to take to get the company moving. Sometimes there is a problem between partners in a business; one wants to make some positive moves and the other is reluctant to do so. In such situations, suggest working with the client in making a study of the long-range possibilities of the company. Such a study will cause the client to start some serious thinking about his long-range goals. It will get him off "dead center." The study might involve interviews with the client, his banker, his lawyer, his stockholders, his customers, his employees, obtaining information about the company and its future potential.

Subjects to be reviewed would concern the company's physical facilities, its personnel, the geographic and product areas in which it is presently serving and potential areas for expansion. It would encompass the need for additional capital or other financing.

Such a study would require some hard thinking on the part of the accountant as to where the future of the company lies. He would prepare a written report, possibly with several drafts reflecting different stages of the study.

While this service may seem far afield from the practice of accounting, the accountant is usually the client's closest advisor, knows more about the business than any other outsider and can motivate the client by helping him with such a study.

Studies on Weakness in Profit Structure

A poor profit structure is usually caused by one of the following; inadequate sales volume, inadequate pricing or high expenses. The client may be accepting poor results as normal without taking initiative to locate the cause and take corrective action. The accountant can motivate the client and get him off "dead center" in this area also. If gross profit margins appear to be too low, the accountant can test his pricing by studying what competitors are charging for the same merchandise or service. If expenses are out of line, special studies can be made of particular areas to determine why costs are high and what can be done about it. If sales volume is low, the accountant can talk to customers or former customers to find out if there are problems in service, delivery or type of merchandise. If he does the job properly, the accountant can come up with valuable facts and recommendations. Just as important, however, is the motivation of the client by bringing this matter "on to the front burner," requiring him to think about it and make plans to solve his problems.

Bringing Together Clients Who Could Help Each Other

The accountant sometimes will find that two clients could help each other and are not aware of it. The clients may find it to their advantage to do business with each other, or in some cases they might benefit through an ownership affiliation. Two clients might find mutual advantage in going into partnership or it might be advantageous for one client to acquire the other.

The accountant is in a unique position to bring together clients who could benefit by doing business with each other and should be alert to do so whenever the opportunity presents itself.

Advice on Buying or Selling a Business

It is customary for a client who is planning to sell out or to purchase a business to consult his accountant. The usual advice requested relates to the tax effect of the transaction.

Accountants are also frequently consulted regarding how much a business is worth to a prospective buyer or seller. The client should be advised that there are different ways to value a business enterprise. The most frequently used are: (1) a valuation based on the physical assets of the company; (2) a valuation based on the earning power of the company. If the physical assets are to provide the basis for the selling price, it is necessary to have them evaluated or appraised. If the price is based upon earning power, the practitioner can prepare computations of the return on investment that a prospective buyer could expect, based on various prices and levels of earnings. You can provide a useful service by making these computations and presenting your findings in a suitable letter report.

Helping the Client Locate "Hidden Costs"

A number of factors in the operation of a business can significantly increase costs but are not readily identifiable on the operating statement. One of these is the cost of personnel turnover. Any experienced client will certainly be cognizant that excessive turnover in personnel is expensive. The cost of recruiting, interviewing and training new people runs very high. Frequently, it is to the employer's advantage to provide additional benefits to capable employees in order to minimize personnel turnover.

The client may not realize the amount of personnel turnover that he has or the cost involved. The accountant can make a simple study of this matter by reviewing the W-2 forms and comparing them with the number of company employees. If this indicates an excessive employee turnover, the matter can be studied in more depth by trying to identify why turnover is high.

The practitioner can further help the client by reviewing the cost of maintaining the company systems of controls and comparing these costs with the results obtained. Many clients spend significant sums in checking both incoming and outgoing invoices, checking payrolls, maintaining perpetual inventory systems and the like. Such systems are valuable and necessary and, indeed, are generally recommended by accountants. The cost of maintaining such controls, however, must be kept in mind.

The accountant can review the procedures for checking incoming invoices to determine if only invoices which have potential for errors are being checked. The checking of arithmetic on small invoices, invoices of reputable suppliers of long standing or invoices which have been prepared by data processing equipment generally is not very productive.

The most important control feature regarding sales invoices pertains to seeing that the company is billing for all merchandise shipped. The potential for significant losses is much higher here than it is with errors in arithmetic. A review of company controls regarding billings is, therefore, quite important.

If the company maintains perpetual inventory records, review the use to which these records are put. The company should be using them for ordering purposes. In addition, the records may be used for controlling inventory accuracy and checking against theft. If the latter is the primary purpose, items of low value or small volume could possibly be eliminated, thus concentrating on high volume and high value items which have more potential for loss.

Customer dissatisfaction can be a major cost and is a hidden cost. A review of certain accounts such as sales returns and accounts receivable can reveal clues to these important items. Sales returns is an account which often does not receive much attention. Keep in mind, however, that every entry to this account arises from some type of customer problem. A careful analysis of the charges can provide clues as to such problem areas as defective merchandise, delayed shipments, and poor service.

An analysis of the accounts receivable ledger will reveal customers who have reduced their activity or discontinued doing business with the company. Here again, a review of this material provides a fertile field for developing material regarding poor customer service and the hidden cost of lost sales. While the accountant should not attempt to perform market surveys, which is a field of its own, he could be of assistance by conducting some interviews with former customers and dissatisfied customers. Discussions with customers concerning the reason for returned sales could give a valuable insight into such problems.

Another hidden cost is cash discounts not taken. If this situation exists the amount of discounts missed should be determined. If the information is not available, consider providing in the accounting system a procedure whereby discounts not taken are segregated into a separate expense account. Once the company is made aware of this hidden cost, they are then in a better position to determine what steps to take.

Special Audits

There is a surprising lack of special-purpose auditing on the part of many accounting firms. There is a tendency to feel that either a full audit must be performed or no auditing at all. As a matter of fact, there are many special audits that are of benefit to clients.

An audit of cash transactions is generally required upon suspicion of embezzlement. Such audits should be performed, as preventive medicine, more frequently than they are. A special examination of the cash controls and cash transactions can generally be done at a cost which is well-worth the effect it has on employees who handle cash. The client should be cautioned, however, that such an audit is not a guarantee against embezzlement.

Confirmation of accounts receivable is a procedure that could be suggested from time to time. Such confirmations keep employees on their toes and sometimes cause customers to be more prompt in paying their accounts.

A physical observation of the client's inventory assures that the inventory count has been reasonably taken and that the merchandise as stated is physically present. The inventory procedure should also include a subsequent check to see that the inventory is fairly priced. This special audit procedure could be of value to certain clients.

Competence

It is appropriate to conclude this discussion with some comments on competence in the management services area. This is a specialized field which requires knowledge and aptitude. The practitioner should take advantage of courses offered by the professional accounting societies. He very likely will want to join organizations which direct their efforts toward management problems and education. He needs to develop a reference library which will give guidance in this area of practice. Other sources of education can be developed, such as salesmen for data processing equipment companies.

Nothing can destroy the reputation of an accountant as quickly as an incompetent job. In special services work, the practitioner's efforts are usually highly visible and the results easy to evaluate by the client. Before you jump in, therefore, be sure you have the competence to do the job.

Index

Index

215